Unreal

J A M E S   S E R V E N

PAGE PUBLISHING
Conneaut Lake, PA

First originally published by Page Publishing 2024

ISBN 979-8-89315-013-1 (pbk)
ISBN 979-8-89315-030-8 (digital)

Printed in the United States of America

"Unreal"

I am the sole survivor of a tragic airplane crash in 1978 in the San Bernardino National Forest in California. Here is my story...

Life is full of stories. They are what make us who we are and shape our lives. There are many stories in my life that have connections to my 1978 plane crash. That was the most intense, harrowing, and tragic event in my life. But life has been full of other stories too. There is a serious side to life and a lighter side to life. So here are many, many other adventures, anecdotes, and memorable events. Some are funny. Some are tragic. Some are ironic. Some are short. Some are long. But I am hoping that all are interesting...and a little bit unreal.

I truly believe that you can get through anything life throws at you. I also believe that you can do anything and be anything you want to be. I wanted to recover from my life-threatening and debilitating injuries, be able to walk again, and play sports again, and I did!

I had an acquaintance in high school who wanted to be a NASA astronaut (unheard of ambition from someone from the small blue-collar town of Temple City). That student, Steve Lindsey, became a NASA astronaut and made many flights around the earth! The rest of my examples will be explained in the stories that follow. I had an "assistant coach" at University High School in Irvine who wanted to be an actor/comedian. Wait until you see how that turned out. I had a basketball player of mine at Palm Desert High School tell me that he wanted to be an actor. What a great story! My referee partner said he wanted to be an "NBA ref." He sent me tickets to a couple of his games when he made it to the NBA. Lastly, I had a five-year-old boy tell me he wanted to be a Major League Baseball player. Twenty-two years later, he made his MLB debut in Denver for the Rockies. Never give up or give in.

I have been a teacher for thirty-five years and a high school coach for forty years. I have a Bachelor's Degree in exercise physiology from Long Beach State University and a Master's Degree in education from California State University at San Bernardino. I have earned numerous teacher's credentials (including multiple-subject, math, and science credentials). I have taught and/or coached at numerous schools throughout Southern California, including schools in Orange County, Los Angeles County, and Riverside County. The majority of my career (more than thirty years) has been spent teaching at Palm Desert High School in Palm Desert and Horizon School in La Quinta. I have been coaching at Palm Desert High School since 1992.

In the early years of my career, I was lucky enough to teach and coach at some great places. Here is a list of schools I have taught and/or coached at over the years: University High School in Irvine, La Quinta High School in Westminster, Los Amigos High School in Fountain Valley, Garden Grove High School in Garden Grove, Ocean View High School in Huntington Beach, Washington Middle School in Pasadena, Temple City High School in Temple City, Arroyo High School in El Monte, Rosemead High School in Rosemead, Bishop Amat High School in La Puente, Desert Springs Middle School in Desert Hot Springs, and my last destinations of Palm Desert High School and Horizon School.

I was lucky enough to meet and coach with some truly legendary mentors/coaches. Some of these legendary mentors and coaches include Steve Scoggin (basketball coach at University High School), Rainer

Wolf (basketball coach at University High School and a CIF administrator), Lee Jackson (basketball coach at University High School), Kevin Reynolds (basketball coach at University High School), Gary McKnight (basketball coach at Mater Dei High School), Jim Harris (basketball coach at Ocean View High School), Dave Demarest (baseball coach at La Quinta High School), Gene McCreadie (basketball coach at Temple City High School), Dennis Marquardt (baseball coach at Temple City High School), Rob Voors (baseball coach at Temple City High School), Bob Sorenson (basketball coach at Arroyo High School), Mike Gorball (basketball coach at Arroyo High School), Richard Wiard (basketball coach at Bishop Amat High School), Don Brady (basketball coach at Palm Desert High School), Darol Salazar (baseball coach at Palm Desert High School), Carol Cox (basketball and softball coach at Palm Desert High School), Christina Osborne (softball coach at Palm Desert High School), Dennis Zink (basketball coach at Palm Springs High School), Henry Viveros (basketball coach at Indio High School and College of the Desert), Rob Hanmer (basketball coach at Rancho Mirage High School), Danielle Oswood (basketball and softball coach at Palm Desert High School), Ken Simonds (basketball coach at Palm Valley High School and

Copper Mountain College), Garrett Estrin (softball and soccer coach at College of the Desert and soccer coach at Hawaii Hilo University), and one of my greatest mentors, my older brother, Bob Serven (basketball coach at Newport Harbor High School, Costa Mesa High School, Edison High School, and Mater Dei High School). These are just some of the people who have helped me along the way.

STORIES

These stories range from trips to Australia, New Zealand, Mexico, Florida, Cooperstown, and even Angel and Laker games. There are other stories about other trips and misadventures. There are stories about coaching, weddings, skiing trips, refereeing high school basketball games, going out with buddies on weekends, and other misadventures with friends.

Preflight and Airplane Crash

It was February 12, 1978, and it was an ordinary Sunday in Temple City, California, a small working-class bedroom community twenty miles or so east of Los Angeles. It was President's Weekend, and so I was just lying around, reading the Sunday paper, when a neighbor, Randy Dowling, an seventeen-year-old who had had his pilot's license since he was sixteen, called up and asked if I was interested in being the fourth person and passenger on an airplane that was going to fly from El Monte Airport to a number of local airports to put up posters for an "airplane wash," similar to a car wash. Randy belonged to the Civil Air Patrol, a club for airplane aficionados.

It was the weekend after my sophomore basketball season ended. I was the starting point guard on Temple City High School's sophomore basketball team and had a two-day break before baseball started on Monday, so with nothing else to do, I said I'd love to go. My mother was against the idea and asked me what would happen if we crashed. I, being a sarcastic teenager, said I would carry a parachute with me and jump at the appropriate time. My father was okay with me going, so they reluctantly agreed and gave me some money, which my mom made sure was in quarters so that she could get her opinion across that I shouldn't be going.

They drove me to El Monte Airport, which was a few miles from my house. When I got to the airport, the anticipation was growing, and I was very excited but apprehensive about my first airplane flight, commercial or small plane, which is what we were going to be going in. The airplane was a little four-seater Grumman Cheetah. I met the other three passengers at the airport. The pilot was Randy Dowling. One of the other passengers was a senior star football player at Temple City High School who was a big man on campus. He had a reputation as a great guy. His name was David Emma. His uncles were the local umpires at Temple City National Little League, where my family had played Little League. The fourth passenger beside me was a girl from a local high school known as Bishop Amat High School in La Puente. Her name was Kathleen Taylor. She was sixteen years old.

Taking off was fun and exciting. We were on our way to an airport in Colton, where we landed, put up posters, took off again to another airport, and did that again until we reached our farthest destination, which was Apple Valley, up in the high desert. We got lunch and had a good time hanging out together. I remember Randy getting on the payphone and making a phone call, which turned out to be a call to find out how the weather was. A major, major storm was forecast (unbeknownst to me), and it is on record as one of the worst storms and winters in the history of Los Angeles. The storm occurred on February 12–13, 1978. It was on its way toward us, but it was not supposed to hit us until four or five hours after we would have returned back to El Monte Airport.

We figured out our seating. I sat at the back left, behind the pilot, and we took off for our flight back to El Monte Airport. Unfortunately, on the way back to El Monte Airport, I noticed that we were starting to fly into a lot of clouds. At first, there were thin clouds and then eventually very thick clouds, whereas I couldn't even see the wing of the airplane, which was probably two feet from my seat. At this point, I became somewhat scared and asked the pilot, Randy, how everything was going. I asked if we were okay, and he assured me that he had lots of experience flying in inclement weather and that this was just a temporary cluster of clouds. We would be through them very soon. After some time had gone by, the clouds stayed just as bad, and I was starting to get very scared. At some point, the pilot started radioing in, sounding somewhat concerned. I was listening closely to his radio communications about what the weather was like and that we were in trouble. And at one point, I heard the term "Mayday"! I knew, even at my young age, that it was not a good thing to hear when you're on a trip in an airplane, boat, or whatever.

We continued flying for what seemed like hours. In reality, it was probably only about half an hour or so. We finally got through some of the clouds into a more open area, which turned out to be the ravine of a mountain range where we flew around for, once again, seemed like an interminable amount of time, but I didn't realize that we were slowly getting lower and lower as we circled, with the engine sounding less and less powerful and cutting out, almost like when a car runs out of gas. It was putting along (that's how I was hearing the engine), and I was feeling very scared. Eventually, the pilot told us, in a hysterical but understandable declaration, that we were going to crash. The girl next to me was praying, which really scared me. The other passenger, David, was trying to help Randy do some kind of evasive maneuver to possibly help us not crash. The last thing I truly remember was hitting something (it turned out to be a very massive tree) while we were circling above the ground, flying lower and lower. We crashed at about 5:00 p.m.

The next memory I have is of being thrown around in such a violent and out-of-control way, as to compare it to being hit by a wave at the beach and being turned over and over, not knowing what was up or what was down. I assume that was the actual crash that occurred after our plane hit a towering tree and slingshotted us pretty much straight down into the ground at a ninety-degree angle. When the plane was discovered the next day, it was stuck straight up and down into the ground, which was because we were stuck into a two-foot-wide, jagged, broken tree stump, which we impacted on the ground. The plane crumbled under the immense pressure of the impact, and the tree stump pierced the metal of the plane, driving itself through the metal of the airplane.

The twenty-four-hour ordeal was in below-zero-degree weather. At some point, it was approximately fifteen degrees below (which included the windchill factor). The time from the actual crash until being rescued was about twenty-four hours. The night I spent there was harrowing and very scary. I was seemingly knocked unconscious from the crash. The time from the crash until daybreak the next morning was a time of vague memories, unusual memories, and possibly true memories. I do "remember" Kathy complaining about the horrible pain in her head. That does seem possible. She had massive head injuries, and I was told later that she probably did survive for a time. I remember Randy complaining about incredible stomach pain. That also seems plausible with him sustaining massive internal injuries. He was saying his seat belt was too tight. That all makes sense to me, but I can't and never will be sure those things ever occurred. Sadly, I never heard David. He was impacted by the jagged tree stump that pierced the plane right at the spot where he was seated, and the unimaginable happened—he had his legs severed from his body and passed away immediately. Yes, I woke up to this nightmare. It was very, very cold, and I remember that during the pitch-black night, I was yelling to my mom to turn the heater up. How I survived the night, I will never understand.

Then the next thing I knew, it must have been 5:00 or 6:00 a.m. I started to see shapes in the distance, but it sure was cold. The shapes turned out to be trees and plants in the mountains. There was snow everywhere. I could slowly make out what was around me, and at that moment, I became totally cognizant of what had happened and what my new horrible situation was. As I noticed the bodies around me, I did notice that my leg was at a strange angle. I reached down, and as I touched my right shin, I felt the bones from my lower leg sticking out from the inside of my leg. Also, my hip was hurting pretty bad too. My right hip bone had become dislocated out of my hip joint. There was blood everywhere. My right foot was still in my shoe, but it was completely covered by my blood, coming out of the compound fracture in my lower leg. I always describe it as looking like a blood ice cube.

Amazingly, I was totally awake and conscious of where I was, what had happened, and what a bad situation I was in. I looked to see if the radio was still able to work, but it was pretty much smashed up and seriously damaged. I thought about my escape, but I couldn't really move much. By the way, Randy was still breathing, but his breaths were very shallow and very labored. I couldn't do anything to help him. Kathy had passed away by the time I woke up in the morning. I thought about trying to crawl away, but then I thought about that movie about the soccer team that crashed in the Andes, and some of those guys just disappeared in the snow when they walked away from their downed plane. So I decided to stay put (not that I could have really gone anywhere). And where was I, actually? I had no idea. I found a map in the plane, and I thought that was good news. But how did that help me? I still didn't know where I was.

The one night I was there went by relatively quickly. Probably because I was knocked out and going in and out of consciousness. So the next day, I did fall asleep a number of times while sitting in the plane, waiting and hoping that someone was looking for me and was trying to rescue me. I don't think it was actual "sleep." I was probably going in and out of consciousness again. I had lost a lot of blood. The day was slow, but a few hours later (I can never be sure of time), I heard the most joyous sound I ever heard—an airplane flying over! They were looking for me! But the plane just kept on flying by. I did notice that the airplane I was in was green and white. That was the same color as the snow and the trees. It was the best camouflaged plane ever. What I didn't know was that there was some kind of transponder that sent out a signal as to the general area of our whereabouts. After numerous other flyovers by planes and numerous times of them just flying over and continuing away from me, I did start to kind of give up on them rescuing me. But, strangely enough, I NEVER actually thought I was going to die! Now when we were still in the air before the crash and we knew we were going to crash, I did think *I am going to die.* I was thinking I was fifteen years old, and I was going to be dead any minute. It was hard to grasp. But once I woke up from the crash, I never again thought about dying. I am still amazed by that.

Hours after the last plane had flown by, I was just sitting there when I heard another great thing—a helicopter was in the air just off to the side of the plane hovering over us. A person on a loudspeaker was talking to me, asking me if I was okay.

I had never been so happy! I motioned to the helicopter that I had a broken leg by doing a snapping motion with my hands. The pilot said, "Okay, we will be right back." And they took off. What? They took off.

After the helicopter departed, I had second thoughts about whether or not what had just happened was even real. I thought I was possibly hallucinating and figured that there was no way a rescue helicopter would leave me there, and considering that the loudspeaker was somewhat distorted, I figured that it was a dream or hallucination, and I once again felt helpless and hopeless. But I still never thought that I was going to die.

So I sat there for what seemed like a few more hours, and the next thing I knew, I heard voices coming up behind the airplane, and, once again, a great feeling came over me. It was the San Bernardino rescue people who were there to rescue me.

When the rescue guys got to me, I was under the belief that I had been in the wreckage for at least four or five days, and I told them that I needed something to eat because I was starving. They kind of giggled and said no to food, but said they could give me some water. I had already thought about eating snow, which was water, but then I remembered laughing to myself about eating the snow. My dad always had this license plate frame on his car that read, "Don't Eat Yellow Snow."

Now that I have been a high school coach for forty years, I think back to the next question I asked my rescuers. I use this mindset when I am explaining to my athletes that commitment and zeal for sports and life are so important and necessary to be successful in sports and in life. As I was laying there with a shattered tibia and fibula, a dislocated hip, frostbite, cuts, and bruises, I asked (very seriously, mind you), "Do you guys think there is any way I can make it to my baseball practice?" (The practice was the next day.) Once again, they laughed and said they didn't think so, but they told me, "Maybe."

They surveyed the situation and told me that the helicopter had to drop them off and take off because of the severity of the storm. They stayed with me for a couple of hours, and at this point, it was nearly 4:00 or 5:00 p.m., and it was starting to get dark, which meant another night in twenty below temperatures, which probably, unbeknownst to me, would be the end of my life. The rescue people gave me a down jacket that was so comfortable and warm. As for themselves, I was later told they almost lost their lives in those freezing, snowy conditions. Somewhere around 5:00 p.m., the rescue people got up and told me that they were going to grab me by the arms. They asked me if I could hold onto their shoulders as they were going to get me to the helicopter, which had just landed a hundred yards or so away in a clearing. I didn't argue, and I tried to hold on to the shoulders. But I didn't have the strength, so they pretty much just dragged me along the ground with a flopping broken leg and a hip dislocation, causing great pain. They did stop after a little distance and wrap my legs together with a blanket that they used as a splint so that my leg wasn't flopping around so much. The helicopter ride was the most comfortable ride I've ever had the good fortune to take. One thing I do remember for sure, and I am still amazed by it, was that one of my rescuers was named Ron…Hazard. What were the odds? On to Loma Linda Hospital…

I remember floating through the air in the helicopter, sitting in the warmth and comfort on my way to…I didn't know where. It turned out I was on my way to the roof of Loma Linda University Hospital in Loma Linda, California.

I remember the helicopter landing on the roof, and then after we landed, all hell broke loose. People were frantically running all over the place. They put me on a gurney and pushed me into an emergency room, where they checked on all my injuries. I'm not sure in what order things were done, but in no particular order, the emergency staff irrigated out my right leg, set both broken bones, and put my dislocated hip bone back into place. All of these procedures hurt a lot.

The other thing that occurred, which was really strange, was that the pilot's parents came into the ER, and when they saw that it was me, they collapsed in tears. It turned out that the parents (who were all in a vigil at the San Bernardino rescue headquarters) were told that the injured passenger was being transported to the hospital, but because they weren't sure which passenger it was, all of the parents were told to wait until they got word as to the injured person's identity. But the pilot's parents must have assumed that it was their son, so they went to the hospital anyway. They were to be disappointed when they saw that it wasn't their son. So it made sense when later I saw my younger brother come into the ER, look at me, and then leave and go outside and tell my parents that it was indeed me. Then my parents came in and saw me.

I spent fourteen days in intensive care. I was put on a gurney a number of times, and I was on my way to surgery to try to save me from contracting gangrene. The cold weather had done quite a number on my feet and toes. Frostbitten and numb, I was taken into surgery to first have my leg amputated, which thankfully never happened. I was also prepped to have my feet and toes amputated. Thankfully, neither of these things ever occurred. My right leg, foot, and toes were in bad shape. The blood had, in essence, made my right foot a blood ice cube. But without the cold, I probably would have bled to death. They put a cast on my right leg up to my hip, and approximately fourteen days later, I was brought home in a wheelchair. I remember that I did have my very own priest or minister who was a constant visitor. My mom told me later that he was there to help me with the trauma and "read me my last rites" if I wasn't going to survive. I never knew if that was true. He sure looked a lot like the singer, John Denver. Ironically, John Denver passed away in a plane crash.

Once home, I had my bed set up in the living room of our small house. I had trouble getting around, but my mom was there to take care of me every day. Up until her death in 2011, she called me every February 13 to tell me that she loved me and how happy she was that I had survived.

I was homeschooled for the remainder of that school year. My teacher was a great guy. He was a music teacher who knew nothing about math. So I had to teach myself advanced algebra. Maybe that's what led me to get a math credential as a teacher later in my life. I was very much into sports, and I would go throw off the pitcher's mound at the local baseball field even with my cast on. I never thought that I would not play sports again, even though a doctor had mentioned that I might never walk again, and even if I did, I wouldn't ever play sports again.

Eventually, I kept getting smaller casts, and about ten months of being on crutches came to an end, and I started walking again. I didn't do any kind of therapy (either physical or mental). It was 1978, and those things weren't big back then. I did a lot of stuff on my own, and even though I wasn't allowed to play football or basketball in my junior year because of the pounding on my leg, I did make the baseball team and played in numerous games.

Before my senior year, I was determined to make the varsity basketball and baseball teams. I worked very hard in the summer and ended up earning the starting point guard position at Temple City High School and being one of the top players on the varsity baseball team, where I earned All-League honors as an outfielder.

After high school, I decided to attend the local community college, Pasadena City College (PCC), and played some baseball there. In the summer after my senior year, I played on the local high-level Senior Babe Ruth baseball team. It was at a team gathering that summer where a local girl came to our team party, and after meeting her, I knew she was going to be my wife someday. After a few years of adventure in my life, which included taking baseball teams to Australia, New Zealand, Fiji, Hawaii, and Tahiti during numerous summers, we reconnected, and Laura has been my wife for over thirty years! More on that later.

Overcoming Injuries

I have been told the impact of our crash into a jagged and practically immovable tree stump would have been like crashing a car going one hundred miles per hour into a brick wall. After impact and being thrown around the plane, I somehow ended up back in my original seat in the plane, but I was sitting on the back rest and leaning back onto the seat portion. I knew pretty quickly after becoming conscious that my lower right leg was broken in half with the bones sticking out of my skin (a compound fracture). I also felt that my hip bone was not in its correct place, causing terrible pain in that area.

After being transported to the hospital, being treated, and eventually discharged fourteen days later, I had to deal with these injuries and work to overcome whatever repercussions they would bring to me for the rest of my life. Because of the fracture of my tibia and fibula in my right leg, that leg was always going to be one full inch shorter than my left. One of the biggest issues I had to overcome was the problem with "frostbite." My feet (especially the right one because it was the "blood ice cube") were numb for numerous weeks. The doctors kept telling me that when the feeling came back, it would be very painful. I didn't believe them because they didn't hurt at all…at the time. But when the feeling and circulation did start coming back…oohhh, they were correct! It was like the tingling you get when you lay on your arm, and it "goes asleep" for a minute or two. The resulting tingling is bothersome, annoying, and a little bit painful. But when your feet are numb for six to seven weeks, the pain is no longer "tingling" or "a little bit painful." It felt like someone was hitting nails into my feet with a hammer, sometimes twenty-four hours a day. This is absolutely the worst pain I have ever felt. I still don't know how I made it through. And in 1978, when I was fifteen years old, I didn't take any pain medications to mask or kill the excruciating pain. I still have trouble when I go to cold regions. My feet get numb quicker than normal.

I worked so hard so that I could continue my sports career. I started walking and running long distances. I had special lifts made for my right shoe. I started lifting weights. As stated, I ended up being an all-league player on the varsity baseball team and a starter on the varsity basketball team. I continued to play multiple sports after high school and college. I ran a couple of half-marathons at the Rose Bowl in Pasadena, California. I completed numerous mini-triathlons in Southern California and continued to ride my bike on long rides over the years.

Final Radio Transmission and Deposition

Approximately 18 months after my plane crash (August of 1979) I was asked to give a deposition in regards to the details and events of that fateful day. This deposition was related to some legal matters which were occurring at that time.

Before you read the deposition, here is the transcript from the final radio transmission between the air traffic controllers at an airport in Ontario and our pilot:

3

2322:22	PO	yes sir one two four point eight for four two uniform
2322:26	42U	one two four point eight four two uniform roger thank you very much
2322:27	RD	cheetah four two uniform ontario how do you hear me
2322:35	RD	cheetah four two uniform ontario approach if you hear me ident
2322:42	42U	ontario radio this is nine eight four two uniform over
2322:47	RD	cheetah nine eight four two uniform ontario approach how do you hear me
2322:51	42U	loud and clear (unintelligible) were having some turbulence here go ahead
2322:55	RD	four two uniform roger say your altitude
2322:59	42U	ah er ah uh almost uh descending uh down to seven thousand now
2323:06	RD	cheetah four two uniform roger suggest heading one six zero one six zero maintain v f r if feasible ontario if v f r visibility four miles light rain wind three five zero at eight altimeter two niner niner two what are your flight conditions
2323:26	RD	cheetah four two uniform caution youre in a area of high terrain up to one two thousand are you in v f r conditions
2323:46	RD	cheetah four two uniform ontario
2323:51	42U	four two uniform were here ahm we saw the high terrain were climbing climbing can you get us any radar please

CONTROL

4

2323:58	RD	four two uniform affirmative uh ident please and ah you are in an area of high terrain are you in v f r conditions now
2324:07	42U	(unintelligible) negative negative negative
2324:13	RD	four two uniform roger climb and maintain ah eight thousand maintain eight thousand heading correction climb and maintain one three thousand
2324:35	RD	cheetah four two uniform id suggest flying heading one zero zero one zero zero
2324:58	RD	cheetah four two uniform how do you hear me
2325:02	42U	uh we hear okay over uh
2325:04	RD	four two uniform roger climb and maintain one three thousand one three thousand and ident on the transponder when you get a chance
2325:36	RD	cheetah four two uniform squawk code zero two six four and ident
2326:05	RD	cheetah four two uniform how do you hear me
2326:08	42U	loud and clear over ahm were we have mountains all around us we can sorta see and ah were i f r ah (unintelligible) we need some help (unintelligible)
2326:19	RD	four two uniform youre transmitters breaking up say your heading and your altitude
2326:30	RD	cheetah four two uniform say your heading and your altitude
2326:49	RD	cheetah four two uniform say your heading and your altitude over

23

Here is a copy of the original document of that deposition: Please note that the first name on the document cover page is incorrect. It should say James Everett Serven. Robert is my brother (and it's my father's name too). Keep in mind I was a 16-year-old boy dealing with this stuff...

JAMES E. SERVEN

SUPERIOR COURT OF THE STATE OF CALIFORNIA

FOR THE COUNTY OF LOS ANGELES

ORIGINAL

𝔇eposition of

ROBERT EVERETT SERVEN

𝔇ate

AUGUST 3, 1979

No. 0897

1

[redacted]
[redacted]
[redacted]
[redacted]
[redacted]
[redacted]

JAMES EVERETT SERVEN,

having been duly sworn, testified as follows:

EXAMINATION

[redacted]

Q   State your full name for the record.

A   James Everett Serven.

Q   What is your age?

A   Sixteen.

Q   What is your date of birth?

A   October 2nd.

Q   What year?

A   1962.

Q   What is your current home address?

A   9839 Daines Drive, Temple City.

Q   Who do you live with there?

A   My mom and dad and my brothers.

2

Q   Do you go to school?

A   Yes. Temple City High School.

Q   What grade?

A   I'm going to be a senior.

Q   This next semester?

A   Yes.

Q   Have you ever had your deposition taken before?

A   No.

Q   I just want to make sure you understand what a deposition is. First, you have been sworn by the gentleman here who is a certified shorthand reporter, an officer of the court. That oath is the same oath you would take if you were testifying in a court of law. You are under the same obligation to tell the truth today under penalty of perjury. Do you understand that?

A   Yes.

Q   The reason we are here today is because there was a plane crash or accident on February 12, 1978 in which I believe you were involved. Is that correct?

A   Yes.

Q   I'm going to be asking you questions about what happened, your relationship with the other people that were in the plane and generally what you know about the crash and the facts surrounding the accident. It's important we get your best responses from what you now remember and recollect about the accident. We don't want you to guess. We don't want you to speculate. We want to know just what you know, no more, no less. So, if I ask you a question you don't understand, don't answer it, just simply say you don't know or understand the question and

1 I'll rephrase the question. Okay?

2   A   Yes.

3   Q   If you don't know the answer to any of my questions,

4 simply tell me you don't know the answer. All right?

5   A   Yes.

6   Q   Everything that's being said in this room today is

7 being taken down by the court reporter. Later, his notes will

8 be transcribed into a deposition booklet. This is a typewritten

9 booklet something like a magazine. In order to make sure every-

10 thing that's said is taken down, it's important all of us here

11 speak audibly in words of the English language in answer to any

12 question. Try to avoid just simple nods of the head or responses

13 such as uh-huh or huh-uh because it's hard to take those down

14 and it's impossible to take down a nod of the head or shake of the

15 head or waive of the hand. It's difficult to interpret what it

16 means. Okay?

17   A   Yes.

18   Q   Is your mother here in the room today?

19   A   Yes.

20   Q   You understand it's your deposition we're taking and

21 it's your testimony we want and if you don't know an answer,

22 that's what you have to tell us. If you do know the answer, that's

23 what you have to tell us and you can't ask your mother for any

24 assistance. We just want to know what you know about this

25 situation. Okay?

26   A   Yes.

27   Q   Are you under any medication at the present time?

28   A   No.

4

1   Q   Are you in good health?

2   A   Yes.

3   Q   Do you feel okay?

4   A   Yes.

5   Q   No reason why your deposition shouldn't be taken at

6 this time?

7   A   No.

8   Q   Do you have any questions before we go on?

9   A   No.

10   Q   When did you first meet Randall Scott Dowling also

11 known as Randy Dowling?

12   A   He lived down the street when I was younger, about

13 1967, somewhere in there. I don't write down when I meet

14 people. They just lived down the street.

15   Q   Grew up together in the same neighborhood?

16   A   Yes.

17   Q   Did he also live on Daines Drive?

18   A   Yes.

19   Q   Did he live there at the time of this accident?

20   A   Yes.

21   Q   Do you know what his address was?

22   A   No.

23   Q   Did you go to the same schools with Randy Dowling?

24   A   Yes.

25   Q   You weren't in the same grade, were you?

26   A   No.

27   Q   Do you know how old Randy Dowling was at the time of

28 the accident?

5

A   Seventeen.

Q   Was he still in high school at the time?

A   Yeah.

Q   How old were you at the time of the accident?

A   Fifteen.

Q   Were you in high school at that time?

A   Yes.

Q   Did you both attend the same high school?

A   Yes.

Q   What high school was that?

A   Temple City High School.

Q   Do you know when Randy Dowling got his pilot's license?

A   No.

Q   Do you know approximately how long he had been flying airplanes prior to this accident?

A   About a year, I think.

Q   Did you ever fly in an airplane piloted by Randy prior to the date of this accident?

A   No.

Q   Had you ever been in a small plane or single engine aircraft as a passenger before this accident?

A   No.

Q   One other thing, just so the reporter doesn't get mad, it's easier for him to take one of us talking at a time so if you will wait until I finish my question before you answer, the reporter will be happier with us.

A   Okay.

Q   I believe also in the aircraft at the time of the

1   accident was Cathy Lee Taylor and David Emma.

2   A   Yes.

3   Q   Was there anybody else in the airplane?

4   A   Aside from me, no.

5   Q   Just the four of you?

6   A   Yes.

7   Q   How many seats did the plane have?

8   A   Four.

9   Q   Was the pilot seated in the left front seat?

10   A   There was two pilot seats, I mean, controls on both

11 sides.

12   Q   At the time of the accident occurring, was Randy

13 sitting in the left front seat?

14   A   Yes.

15   Q   Were you sitting in the left rear directly behind

16 Randy?

17   A   Yes.

18   Q   Was David Emma in the right front seat?

19   A   Yes.

20   Q   Was Cathy Taylor in the right rear seat?

21   A   Yes.

22   Q   This accident happened on a weekday or weekend?

23   A   On Sunday.

24   Q   Again, I don't want you to guess or speculate. If

25 you think it happened on a Sunday, that's what I'm entitled to.

26   A   Yes.

27   Q   How did it come about that you went on this trip with

28 Randy?

1   A   He called me up and asked me if I wanted to go.

2   Q   Did he tell you he was going somewhere?

3   A   He said we were going to fly somewhere for lunch and

4   fly back.

5   Q   He called you up the same day?

6   A   Yes.

7   Q   Did you and Randy belong to any organizations together?

8   A   No.

9   Q   For instance, you weren't in Scouting together?

10   A   No.

11   Q   What time did he call you?

12   A   About 10:00, I think it was. Do you want me like to

13   say if I think it was around 10:00 because I'm pretty sure --

14   Q   Yes.

15   A   Yeah. 10:00 o'clock.

16   Q   As best you remember, what did he say?

17   A   He asked me if I was doing anything and if I wasn't,

18   would I want to be a passenger with him, he was going to go out

19   flying.

20   Q   Did he tell you where he was going to go at that time?

21   A   Not then, but he came down and mentioned Apple Valley.

22   Q   He came down to your house?

23   A   Or when I was going half-way down, I remember seeing

24   him and tell me that.

25   Q   When he called you up and asked if you wanted to go

26   flying, what did you say?

27   A   Yes, because I had never been so I wanted to.

28   Q   Had you talked with him before about going flying?

1   A   No. He told me about flying, but I never really said

2   I wanted to go with him or anything like that.

3   Q   Had you ever met Cathy Lee Taylor before the day of

4   the accident?

5   A   Yes.

6   Q   How about David Emma? Had you ever met him before?

7   A   Yes.

8   Q   Where did you first meet David?

9   A   At little league baseball.

10   Q   About when was that?

11   A   Probably when he was twelve years old or so in the

12   league because my brother was in it with him. I saw him playing

13   and stuff. I never was friends, just knew him.

14   Q   More of a friend of your brother than yours?

15   A   Not too much of a friend of my brother's, but that's

16   how I knew him, my brother being in the league.

17   Q   What is your brother's name?

18   A   Bob.

19   Q   And Bob and David were in the same league?

20   A   Yeah.

21   Q   Same team?

22   A   No. I don't think they're the same age, just around

23   the same time.

24   Q   How old is Bob?

25   A   Nineteen.

26   Q   After Randy called you on the date of the accident,

27   and asked you if you wanted to go flying with him, you agreed

28   to go. Is that correct?

1 A   Yes.

2 Q   What time did you meet Randy after that?

3 A   I don't know exactly.

4 Q   Shortly after that?

5 A   About forty-five minutes or so, somewhere in there.

6 Q   Where did you meet him?

7 A   At his house.

8 Q   Anybody at his house when you went there?

9 A   Well, David picked me up and we just drove down there
10 and just me and David and Randy was there.

11 Q   Did you talk to David before he picked you up?

12 A   No.

13 Q   Randy told you David was going to come by and pick you
14 up?

15 A   No, he just came in on his way to Randy's house.

16 Q   When David picked you up, this was about forty-five
17 minutes after Randy called --

18 A   About that, yes --

19 Q   -- did you know where you were going at that time?

20 A   Yes. Apple Valley.

21 Q   Did David tell you that or did Randy tell you that?

22 A   Randy did. He might have told me on the phone. I
23 don't remember exactly.

24 Q   After you got to Randy's house, did you meet Cathy Lee
25 Taylor in Randy's house?

26 A   No.

27 Q   Did the three of you leave together from Randy's house?

28 A   No.

1   Q   Where did you go from Randy's house?

2   A   I stayed in David's truck and Randy road his motor-

3   cycle there to the airport.

4   Q   Did you follow Randy to the airport?

5   A   Yes.

6   Q   What time did the three of you get to the airport?

7   A   I don't know.

8   Q   Was it before Noon?

9   A   It was probably close to that.

10 Q   Did you and David have any conversations on the way to

11 the airport?

12 A   Nothing I remember.

13 Q   Did you talk at all with either David or Randy about

14 why Randy was going to Apple Valley?

15 A   You mean before we took off?

16 Q   Yes.

17 A   He might have mentioned about -- he already told me

18 that about lunch, that's what I thought he was going to do, have

19 lunch there.

20 Q   Any specific place you were told you were going to

21 have lunch?

22 A   At the Apple Valley Inn.

23 Q   Had you ever been to the Apple Valley Inn before?

24 A   I don't think so.

25 Q   Did you and David and Randy arrive at the airport at

26 the same time?

27 A   Yes.

28 Q   Did David park his vehicle close to where Randy parked

11

1 his motorcycle?

2   A   I don't know where Randy parked his motorcycle because
3 I don't think he parked it in the parking spot, he might have
4 parked it over by the building or something. I don't remember.

5   Q   When did you first meet Cathy Taylor?

6   A   In the building. We all went in the building for
7 something and I just met her there.

8   Q   This was a building at the airport?

9   A   Yes.

10   Q   What sort of building was it? What was in the building?

11   A   That's where he filed his flight plan.

12   Q   Were you with him when he made arrangements to rent
13 the airplane?

14   A   No. I don't know if he rented it there. I wasn't
15 with him right next to him when he was doing it.

16   Q   Was he doing it there that morning when you got there?

17   A   I don't know.

18   Q   What did you do after you got to the airport?

19   A   I went into the building and watched the basketball
20 game on TV.

21   Q   Still with David at that time?

22   A   He was standing up but he wasn't with me or Randy,
23 just standing up like looking around, but he was in the building.

24   Q   Was the TV in the same room Randy was in?

25   A   Yeah, but on the other side.

26   Q   Randy go up to a counter or something and talk to
27 somebody at the counter?

28   A   Yes.

Q   How long did this take place that you were in this room?

A   Ten, fifteen minutes.

Q   Did you hear anything that was said between Randy and the people at the counter?

A   No.

Q   Did you talk with anybody at the airport?

A   Did I?

Q   Yes.

A   No.

Q   After about ten or fifteen minutes, did Randy say you were ready to go?

A   I don't remember he just said that.

Q   Did he indicate that he had been successful in renting the plane?

A   He said, come on, or something and we all just followed him out there.

Q   Where did you follow him to?

A   To where the plane was.

Q   Where was that in relationship to the building you were in?

A   Just outside of -- you know, right outside of it.

Q   There were four of you at this time?

A   Yes.

Q   Was Cathy already at the building when you got there?

A   Yes.

Q   Do you know how she got to the airport?

A   She was in her mom's car when we got there, she was

1 waiting for us when we pulled up in David's car, she was there

2 with her mom already.

3   Q   Did you meet Cathy's mother?

4   A   No.

5   Q   Did Cathy get out of her car after you pulled up?

6   A   Yes.

7   Q   Did you have any conversations at all with Cathy?

8   A   When?

9   Q   At that time.

10   A   No.

11   Q   When you left the building after Randy said, come on,

12 did you go directly to the airplane?

13   A   Yeah.

14   Q   Were seats assigned or did you just grab any seat

15 available?

16   A   We didn't get in the plane right away. He filled it

17 with gas or checked it -- I wasn't watching him that closely.

18   Q   Who was doing that?

19   A   Randy was.

20   Q   He put his own gasoline in the plane?

21   A   I don't know.

22   Q   About how long was it after you got out to where the

23 plane was before you got in the plane?

24   A   Another ten, fifteen minutes, somewhere around there.

25   Q   Did Randy have anything with him when he went out to

26 the plane?

27   A   He had posters, like --

28   Q   What sort of posters?

14

1   A   They were some kind of thing he was going to have,
2   like a car wash, but for planes.
3   Q   Handmade posters?
4   A   Yes.
5   Q   Did Randy tell you anything about them?
6   A   He said we were going to take them to the airport we
7   were going to and put them up there.
8   Q   The airport in Apple Valley?
9   A   Yes.
10 Q   Do you know what the posters said?
11 A   Something about a plane wash.
12 Q   Did Randy ever tell you who was having a plane wash?
13 A   No, because he was in the Civil Air Patrol, so I
14 thought it was for that, that's the only thing I knew he was in.
15 Q   Did Randy tell you he made the posters himself?
16 A   No.
17 Q   Did he tell you who made the posters?
18 A   I don't think so.
19 Q   Do you know if either David or Cathy was in the Civil
20 Air Patrol?
21 A   I don't know for sure, but I don't think he -- they
22 were.
23 Q   Go on.
24 A   I think Cathy was. I think that's where he met her,
25 but I'm not positive about that.
26 Q   David have any posters with him when he went out to
27 the plane?
28 A   No.

39

1 Q   Did Cathy have any posters with her when you first met

2 her in the parking lot?

3 A   She might have, but I don't -- I didn't meet her, I

4 just followed Randy, I didn't know what she was doing, I wasn't

5 watching her, just going with him.

6 Q   Did Cathy have any posters with her when you got to

7 the plane?

8 A   I don't think so, no. I'm pretty sure she didn't.

9 Q   About how many posters did Randy have with him?

10 A   Only had them in a stack so I couldn't count them, he

11 put them in the back of the plane.

12 Q   More than two or three?

13 A   I'm not sure. I didn't look at them that closely.

14 Q   About how big were these posters?

15 A   How do you want -- I don't know.

16 Q   Ten by twelve, twenty by forty?

17 A   Can I show you here on the table? About from here

18 over and pretty good size, like you can see them so you can walk

19 up right next to them and read it.

20 Q   About three feet by three feet?

21 A   Yeah, something like that.

22 Q   Some sort of cardboard material?

23 A   Yes.

24 Q   When was the plane wash to be held? Do you know?

25 A   No.

26 Q   After Randy finished gassing up the plane, did you get

27 into the plane at that time?

28 A   He might have done something else. I mean, whatever

1   he was doing he was done with, then we got in, yeah.

2   Q   When you got in, did anybody tell you where to sit?

3   A   I just got in first so I got in the back.

4   Q   Were the four of you talking about flying at this time

5   or were you pretty quiet?

6   A   We might have been talking about whatever came up,

7   nothing that I remember.

8   Q   When you got in the plane, did Randy make any comments

9   about the trip you were ready to take?

10   A   Not that I remember.

11   Q   Did Randy start the plane up at that time?

12   A   Yeah.

13   Q   And taxied out to the runway?

14   A   We coasted out and he talked to this guy he knew about

15   something.

16   Q   He was talking to somebody else about the plane or

17   on the radio?

18   A   To somebody present there.

19   Q   Do you know what they were talking about?

20   A   No.

21   Q   Was this other person somebody in the Civil Air

22   Patrol?

23   A   I don't know.

24   Q   You don't know who this other person was?

25   A   No.

26   Q   Was it a man?

27   A   Yes.

28   Q   Do you know how old this person was?

1   A   Twenty or so, something like that. Maybe younger.

2   Q   You don't remember anything that was said between

3 Randy and this other person?

4   A   No.

5   Q   Eventually you guys took off. Is that right?

6   A   Yes.

7   Q   Did you hear any clearances from the Tower, ready for

8 takeoff?

9   A   I wasn't listening to anybody, because I had nothing

10 to do with it really. I just was sitting back and enjoying it.

11   Q   Was Randy wearing a headset at this time?

12   A   I don't think he was.

13   Q   Did you see him talking into a radio microphone?

14   A   When?

15   Q   Before you took off.

16   A   I don't remember him talking into one.

17   Q   Did you hear any conversations over the radior at all?

18   A   Yes.

19   Q   Before he took off.

20   A   Yes.

21   Q   Anything that was directed towards Randy or his plane?

22   A   I wasn't listening closely to it.

23   Q   But was there anything that you remember?

24   A   Nothing I remember about it.

25   Q   What was the weather like when you got to the airport

26 that morning before you took off?

27   A   Clear.

28   Q   Was it a warm day?

```
 1    A    Cool day.

 2    Q    How were you dressed?

 3    A    I had a shirt like this and a blue kind of sweatshirt

 4  jacket type thing.

 5    Q    Short sleeve shirt?

 6    A    Yes.

 7    Q    And a sweatshirt jacket over the short sleeve shirt?

 8    A    Yes.

 9    Q    Did you have on jeans?

10    A    Yes.

11    Q    Shoes?

12    A    Yes.

13    Q    Did the other people have jackets also?

14    A    No.  Randy, he might have had one in the plane.  He

15  might have been wearing one.  I don't think he was.  I don't

16  remember.

17    Q    How about David?  Do you know if he had a jacket on?

18    A    No, he didn't.

19    Q    Do you know if Cathy had a jacket with her?

20    A    No, she didn't.

21    Q    Wasn't overcast at all when you took off?

22    A    Not that I remember.  Seemed pretty clear.

23    Q    Blue skies as opposed to a normal hazy gray sky you

24  often see?

25    A    I didn't really, you know, look to see if it was

26  blue.  It wasn't cloudy, it was pretty nice.

27    Q    After you took off, did you fly directly to Apple

28  Valley?
```

19

1   A   Yes.

2   Q   About how long did the flight take?

3   A   Do you want an estimate?

4   Q   Yes. Your best estimate.

5   A   Forty-five minutes. Hour. somewhere in there.

6   Q   Was Randy the only one that was flying the plane
7 during the trip to Apple Valley?

8   A   Might have been on the way back, but I -- he let
9 David take over the control thing just for like five seconds or
10 so.

11   Q   David was sitting in the right front seat?

12   A   Yes.

13   Q   And he also had controls in front of him?

14   A   Yes.

15   Q   Was there anything that appeared to you to be unusual
16 about the flight from El Monte to Apple Valley?

17   A   No.

18   Q   Do you know how high you went up?

19   A   No.

20   Q   Do you remember going over any mountains on the way
21 there?

22   A   No.

23   Q   Was the weather good all the way from El Monte to
24 Apple Valley?

25   A   Yes.

26   Q   Didn't encounter any clouds?

27   A   There were couple real small ones, we'd go by and see
28 them, but real small.

1 Q   What color clouds?

2 A   White, like the clouds when there's a blue sky and

3 little patches of small ones, that's what they were.

4 Q   Were the four of you carrying on any conversation at

5 all during the trip to Apple Valley?

6 A   Nothing, you know, I remember.

7 Q   Do you remember anything that was said during that

8 forty-five minute trip?

9 A   I remember I told Randy to turn up the radio, just

10 small talk and stuff.

11 Q   What was on the radio?

12 A   Music.

13 Q   Listening to an AM channel?

14 A   Yes.

15 Q   Did you talk at all with Cathy on the trip up there?

16 A   No. I think maybe on the way there, she was in the

17 front. I know on the way back David was in the front. I don't

18 -- I was looking out the window most of the time seeing what

19 was down there.

20 Q   Did you enjoy the trip?

21 A   Yes.

22 Q   As you got close to the Apple Valley airport, do you

23 remember if Randy talked with anybody at the airport over the

24 radio?

25 A   I don't remember.

26 Q   Do you remember if Randy talked with anybody over

27 the radio before he landed at Apple Valley?

28 A   I don't remember.

1   Q   You did land at the Apple Valley airport.

2   A   Yes.

3   Q   Did you have lunch at the Apple Valley Inn?

4   A   Yes.

5   Q   Did Randy put up his posters?

6   A   I think he did at the airport. I wasn't watching him

7 all the time.

8   Q   After the plane landed at Apple Valley, he taxied

9 to a stop somewhere. Right?

10   A   Yes.

11   Q   Did you get out at that point?

12   A   Yes.

13   Q   What did you do after that?

14   A   We walked to the, I guess the lobby of the airport.

15   Q   All four of you walked there together?

16   A   No, Randy -- the -- that's where I think he might have

17 put the posters up, stayed back a while and put the posters up

18 and caught up with us.

19   Q   Did you see him put up any of the posters?

20   A   No.

21   Q   Did you see the posters before he put them up?

22   A   No, but I wasn't looking for them.

23   Q   So, you don't know where he put them up.

24   A   No.

25   Q   At some point shortly after you landed were all four

26 of you there together in the lobby?

27   A   Yes.

28   Q   How did you get from the Apple Valley Inn -- from the

22

1 airport to the Apple Valley Inn?

2   A   A man in a van drove us there.

3   Q   Did Randy know this man?

4   A   No, he organized it through the desk or something

5 and it was part of the service or something. It was just wasn't

6 someone's van, it was a service to drive people back and forth.

7   Q   Sort of like an airport transport type thing?

8   A   Yes.

9   Q   How long did you stay at Apple Valley Inn?

10   A   Hour-and-a-half, something. We ate lunch and just

11 went back. I don't know how long it was.

12   Q   All four of you ate lunch together?

13   A   Yes.

14   Q   Do you remember what you had?

15   A   Tuna sandwich, I think, either that or a grilled

16 cheese. I forget exactly.

17   Q   Did you have anything to drink of an alcoholic nature

18 while you were there at the Apple Valley Inn?

19   A   No.

20   Q   Did any of the other people?

21   A   No.

22   Q   Did you ever that day see Randy drink anything of an

23 alcoholic nature?

24   A   No.

25   Q   Did you see anybody else drink anything of an alco-

26 holic nature?

27   A   No.

28   Q   Did you get back to the airport from the Inn by the

47

1   same van that took you?

2   　　A　　Yes.

3   　　Q　　What were you talking about during lunch?

4   　　A　　We weren't talking that much. Eating. I remember I

5   was talking to David about baseball or something for a couple

6   minutes.

7   　　Q　　What time were you expecting to get back to El Monte?

8   　　A　　5:00 or so.

9   　　Q　　When you got back tothe airport from the Apple Valley

10 Inn, what did you do at that time?

11 　　A　　We got in the plane.

12 　　Q　　All four of you?

13 　　A　　I don't think Randy got in right away. I don't know

14 if he did right away. He talked tothe guy in the van for a

15 couple minutes.

16 　　Q　　Did you see Randy talking with anybody else at the

17 airport besides the boy in the van?

18 　　A　　Not that I remember.

19 　　Q　　Did you hear anything that Randy said to the guy in

20 the van?

21 　　A　　No. Not at that time. Earlier, he was talking to

22 them about like property, houses out there on the way back from

23 the Inn. He was asking about how much houses cost and stuff

24 like that. He just was curious.

25 　　Q　　What was the weather like when you got back from the

26 Apple Valley Inn?

27 　　A　　It was windy, but there wasn't a lot of clouds.

28 　　Q　　Still what you would call clear?

1   A   Yes.

2   Q   More cloudy than when you left El Monte?

3   A   I wasn't looking. I figured we'd fly back. I wasn't

4   that concerned about the weather. It wasn't raining so I knew

5   it wouldn't be bad.

6   Q   Was the weather sort of chilly?

7   A   Yes.

8   Q   How long did you sit in the airplane before Randy got

9   in?

10 A   Not very long. Five minutes at the most.

11 Q   No more than five minutes?

12 A   No.

13 Q   After Randy got into the airplane, what did he do?

14 A   I think we took off.

15 Q   Did he start the plane back up again?

16 A   Yes.

17 Q   Did he have to gas it up again?

18 A   I don't think so.

19 Q   After he got back in the airplane, he didn't have to

20 do anything but start the engine?

21 A   That's all I remember, but I wasn't watching him that

22 closely either.

23 Q   He taxied out onto the runway.

24 A   Yes.

25 Q   Did you hear any conversations over the radio Randy

26 was having at this time?

27 A   No.

28 Q   Did you see Randy using the radio at this time?

1   A   No. But, he might have. I just wasn't, you know,

2 watching him.

3   Q   Were there any other planes in the immediate vicinity

4 either taking off or landing?

5   A   When we were waiting for Randy to come back from the

6 van, one plane took off.

7   Q   Same type of plane you were in?

8   A   I guess it was. It looked about the same.

9   Q   Do you know what type of plane you were in?

10   A   It was a Grummand Cheeta.

11   Q   Did you know that as the name --

12   A   He might have mentioned it but I wasn't aware that's

13 what I was in.

14   Q   When Randy took off from Apple Valley airport, where

15 were you headed directly?

16   A   To another airport on the way back to El Monte.

17   Q   What airport was that?

18   A   I don't know. There were two of them we were going

19 to go to and I don't remember which one it was.

20   Q   You planned on stopping at two or three airports

21 before you got back to El Monte?

22   A   Yes.

23   Q   Would you know why he was going to stop at this

24 other airport?

25   A   To put up posters and information about the plane

26 wash.

27   Q   So, when you took off from Apple Valley, did you know

28 at that time what your destination was?

1   Yes.

2   Q   You don't remember what it is now?

3   A   No. It was Rialto airport was one of them we were

4   going to and other airports in that vicinity.

5   Q   Do you remember anybody telling you you were going to

6   the Upland airport?

7   A   That might have been one, yes.

8   Q   But, you don't remember now which one you were headed

9   for directly.

10   A   No.

11   Q   Did there come some point after you took off that you

12   began to be aware of some sort of problem?

13   A   I saw clouds, at first they were just scattered

14   clouds.

15   Q   Did it seem unusual for you to see clouds?

16   A   No.

17   Q   Did anybody make any comments about the fact there

18   were clouds around?

19   A   No.

20   Q   What is the first ting that happened that was unusual

21   as far as you were concerned?

22   A   There was -- when there started to be -- clouds kept

23   getting thicker, you could see less and less as we went along.

24   Q   Did it start getting darker?

25   A   Yes.

26   Q   Did you make any comments about that?

27   A   After a while, I asked Randy if he could get out of

28   it because I don't what a pilot can do, I don't know if it's --

1   he said, yeah, he could get out of it.

2   Q   Were you the first one that spoke up or made a comment?

3   A   David was talking to him, because I was talking to the

4   girl now, but I don't know what they were saying. He might have

5   been talking about it.

6   Q   You didn't hear what he was saying?

7   A   No.

8   Q   About how long after you took off was it you asked

9   Randy about the clouds?

10   A   I don't know. Half an hour. I wasn't occupied with

11   the time. I can't be sure.

12   Q   Wasn't immediately after you took off?

13   A   No.

14   Q   You had been flying for some period of time?

15   A   Yes.

16   Q   As you were flying back from Apple Valley, did you

17   notice going over any mountains?

18   A   We might have, but once the clouds came, I couldn't see

19   anything after that because I was talking most of the time.

20   Q   Did the clouds block your vision of the ground below?

21   A   Not -- clouds at what point?

22   Q   At the point when you made the comment to Randy?

23   A   Partially. Not completely. You could still some.

24   Q   When did Randy first tell you he wasn't going directly

25   from Apple Valley to El Monte?

26   A   I don't remember.

27   Q   Did you know that before you left El Monte?

28   A   I think he told me before we took off, just in case I

28

1 didn't want to go. I'm pretty sure he told me, but I'm not

2 completely sure.

3   Q   Did you ever hear anyone else besides yourself make

4 any comments about the clouds?

5   A   David was talking to him most of the time, but I wasn't

6 listening to them too much. I wasn't listening to what they were

7 saying. They were talking a lot, probably sitting there talking

8 about that.

9   Q   Did Cathy make any comments to you about the weather?

10   A   No.

11   Q   At the time you asked Randy about the clouds, if he

12 could fly out of them, did anybody else appear to be upset or

13 nervous?

14   A   David, he just told me to be quiet.

15   Q   Did the clouds continue to get thicker?

16   A   Yes.

17   Q   Did there come a time when Randy indicated he felt

18 there was some problem?

19   A   When he called in an emergency.

20   Q   About how long after he commented about the clouds

21 was it he called in an emergency?

22   A   Just a couple minutes or so, maybe not. Time was,

23 you know -- I wasn't thinking about that so after I asked him,

24 seemed like pretty soon after that he called in and called an

25 emergency.

26   Q   Do you remember what he said when he called in an

27 emergency?

28   A   We have an emergency.

1   Q   Did he say why?

2   A   No. Not then.

3   Q   Did you ever hear him say why he called an emergency?

4   A   He told them visual something, couldn't see, you know

5 real good, something about visual.

6   Q   Did you ever hear him say he didn't know where he

7 was?

8   A   Well, close to when we crashed, because he was saying

9 a lot of stuff intothe speaker, saying a lot into the -- into

10 the microphone, so he said something, we don't know where we

11 are but that was completely panic and stuff.

12   Q   About how long was it from the time he called in an

13 emergency untilthe time he crashed?

14   A   I've got no idea. Maybe fifteen minutes. Maybe an

15 hour. BecaUse I was kind of worried when he called in an

16 emergency, I had no idea how time there was.

17   Q   After he called in an emergency, did anybody else

18 seem upset?

19   A   David was trying to help him, I guess, talking to him

20 a lot and the girl started praying to me, I guess she was

21 religious and started praying.

22   Q   After Randy called in an emergency, did he ever lose

23 altitude, go back down trying to get underneath the clouds?

24   A   I know we lost a lot but I don't know what he was

25 doing. I remember him saying like don't worry about this or

26 something, don't worry about it, we're going to go down a little

27 bit, but he never said why. I don't know how far he went. He

28 might have gone a short distance but he said something about that.

Q   Did he tell you you couldn't fly over the clouds?

A   He didn't tell me. They just told me -- because they were up in the front and talking about it a lot, just told me to be quiet and stay out of it.

Q   How did the crash happen?

A   Do you want me to say what I know now? Like all the stuff I've learned about it?

Q   Sure. Everything you know now about what happened.

Q   Go ahead and answer.

A   Well, how do you want me to answer it? Like from what I've heard from the other people I've talked to?

Q   First why don't you tell me what you experienced at the time of the crash.

A   Seeing -- We went into like a valley, I remember seeing trees and stuff all around and that's about the last thing I really remember that I can be sure of.

Q   Did there come a point when he realized there was going to be a crash?

A   Yes, when I saw there were trees everywhere, there was a big mountain in front of us, I knew we couldn't get over it, I could figure that out. It was way in front, but I knew we couldn't get over it, that's the last thing I remember and can be sure of.

Q   Did you lose consciousness during the crash?

1   A   I kind of remember being -- it's not -- I'm pretty

2 sure -- it's like when you're in a wave and you just get thrown

3 around, that's what I remember, being thrown all around.

4   Q   Did you hear anybody say anything just before you

5 crashed?

6   A   David was telling Randy to pull up, I guess he meant

7 pull up on the control thing and try to get over it. The last

8 thing I remember Randy saying was we're going to crash and the

9 girl was praying the whole time.

10   Q   Was it raining at the time of the crash?

11   A   I could see -- before the crash, the clouds weren't

12 as bad so I could see the rain, I could see drops and stuff, but

13 I don't remember the rain crashing down like rain drops would.

14 I could tell it was wet.

15   Q   Did you see any ice on the wing?

16   A   No. I just saw water. It could have been ice. It

17 looked like water drops to me.

18   Q   Just before the crash, do you know if the motor was

19 still on?

20   A   I don't remember.

21   Q   Have you learned more about how the crash occurred

22 since the plane crash?

23   A   Yes.

24   Q   Who have you talked to about it since then?

25   A   I've seen pictures of the plane. I've read about it

26 in the newspapers and I've heard like theories of -- I don't

27 remember from whom, it might have been from the people that

28 rescued me. I don't know exactly who, but I've heard it from a

32

lot of different people.

Q   What theories have you heard?

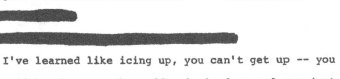

A   I've learned like icing up, you can't get up -- you can't go any higher because the rudder is iced up and you just keep going down and we hit a tree on the left wing and made us spin -- spiral down into a stump. We went into a stump. That was in the pictures, that we just figured we came to a complete stop.

Q   Did you ever hear anybody say whose fault the airplane crash was?

THE WITNESS: I've heard that it was just people have nothing to do with it saying pilot error, something wrong with the pilot. Just anybody?

A   I've heard it could be pilot error, could be weather error, a lot of different things --

57

1

2   Q   ▓▓▓▓▓▓▓▓▓▓   What's the first thing you remember

3   after the crash?

4   A   Kind of being laying down and looking to the side and

5   stuff and seeing a lot of darkness and I thought I was dreaming

6   and I just figured I'd wake up and it wouldn't be there.

7   Q   Do you know what time the plane crash happened?

8   A   I think around 3:30.

9   Q   Do you know what time you were rescued?

10   A   About twenty-four hours later.

11   Q   The next afternoon?

12   A   Yes.

13   Q   You stayed with the plane wreckage for twenty-four

14   hours?

15   A   Yes.

16   Q   Did anybody else survive the crash long enough to say

17   anything to you after the plane crash?

18   A   I don't know if there -- do you want me to tell you

19   this, I wouldn't swear to it, I can swear I know Randy was alive

20   a long time. I remember hearing him breathing, but I can say I

21   think that -- I remember hearing the girl not too much, but say-

22   ing stuff and remembering --

23   Q   Just the best of what you remember.

24   A   Okay. I know Randy lived for a while and I know now

25   that the girl lived but I've kind of a memory that she was talk-

26   ing a little but I don't remember David ever breathing or anything.

27   Q   As far as you know, did Randy ever regain consciousness

28   or say anything to you after the accident?

1   A   The part that I'm not too sure about, I remember him

2 telling me like try to hold him up because he couldn't breath

3 but I know he never really talked after that because I tried to

4 get him to talk and yelling at him and stuff but he wouldn't

5 respond.

6   Q   You say Cathy was talking for sometime, the best you

7 remember, after the accident.

8   A   She was saying some things, I remember her talking

9 but not what she was saying.

10   Q   You don't remember anything she said?

11   A   No, but I know she didn't say anything that was real --

12   Q   Who was it that rescued you from the plane crash?

13   A   You mean who was he or what did he work for?

14   Q   What organization?

15   A   San Bernardino Rescue Squad or something.

16   Q   You received a broken hip and broken leg in the

17 accident?

18   A   No. I got a broken leg and they said I had a bruised

19 hip ███████████████████████████████████████

20 ███

21   Q   Were you also frost bitten?

22   A   Yes.

23   Q   Where did you have frost bite?

24   A   Both feet and both hands but the hands were as bad

25 as the feet.

26   Q   How long did you remain in the hospital after the

27 wreck?

28   A   I think ten days.

Q   While you were in the hosptial, did you talk to any-body about how the accident happened?

A   Some newspapers and some people that were -- I don't know if they were insurance or lawyers. I don't know what they were. They were something. I don't know.

Q   People who said they were investigating the accident?

A   Yes. I guess from National Transportation and Safety Board, something like that.

Q   Did you tell them how the accident happened?

A   You mean what I've told you about it?

Q   Right.

A   Yeah.

Q   Is there anything you remember telling anybody about the accident you haven't told us today?

A   Nothing I can remember. This is everything.

Q   Before you crashed, did you notice anything unusual about the sound of the plane's engine at all?

A   No. I was just, you know, mainly panicked. I wasn't aware of any noise or anything going around me except for the voices.

Q   From the time you teok off from Apple Valley, did you notice anything wrong with the operation of the plane at all?

A   No.

Q   Plane seemed to be functioning okay?

A   Yes.

Q   Did anybody make any comment to you at the time you took off from Apple Valley until you crashed that there was something wrong with the plane?

1   A   No.

2   Q   Did you ever file any lawsuit as a result of the

3 injuries you received in the crash?

4   A   No.

5   Q   Did you ever make any claims against anybody for

6 damages that resulted in injuries you received?

7   A   That's a lawsuit, a claim?

8   Q   A lawsuit is a filing of a piece of paper with the

9 Court against an insurance company or something like that.

10   A   So it would be a claim? Is that the same thing?

11   Q   A lawsuit and claim are not quite the same thing.

12   A   I don't know. I haven't had any of those -- you mean

13 against somebody --

14   Q   Yes.

15   A   No.

16   Q   Did you ever hired a lawyer to represent you?

17   A   No.

18   Q   When was the last time prior to the beginning of your

19 deposition this morning that you talked with anybody about the

20 accident?

21   A   Do you mean a friend and anybody or somebody qualified

22 like an insurance guy or something --

23   Q   Anybody other than your family and close friends.

24   A   Well, I talked like to some people who asked me how

25 did you get hurt because they've seen my leg. You mean anybody?

26   Q   About how the accident happened.

27   A   I talked to a lady one day, talked to her about -- she

28 asked me all about it.

1   Q   Did she tell you she was investigating the accident?

2   A   No, just met her at the doctor's office.

3   Q   When is the last time anybody indicated they were

4   investigating the accident?

5   A   Long time ago. I don't remember because I've talked

6   to people in the hospital and people at my house. I don't

7   remember how long ago it was.

8   Q   Before coming here today, did you read over any docu-

9   ment to refresh your recollection?

10   A   No.

11   Q   Did you look at any pictures?

12   A   No.

13   Q   You talked with people in the Government about how

14   the accident happened. Is that right?

15   A   Do you mean the insurance and like from the National

16   Transportation and SafetyBoard?

17   Q   People from the Safety Board.

18   A   I have before, yes.

19   Q   This is when you were in the hospital?

20   A   I think that was the person who came. He's come to

21   our house and I've talked to him, but that was a long time ago,

22   too.

23   Q   About how long ago did he come to your house?

24   A   To talk to me or just --

25   Q   To talk to you.

26   A   Once maybe twice.

27   Q   When was the last time?

28   A   I don't remember.

Q   Other than the person from the Safety Board, did any-body else talk to you about how the accident happened that said they were investigating the accident?

A   Not that I remember.

Q   Do you know what sort of student Randy was?

A   You mean gradewise? Was he a good student? I don't know exactly. I don't know how good a student he was. I can't be sure.

Q   Was he on any sport teams that you were aware of?

A   No.

Q   Do you know of any organizations he belonged to other than the Civil Air Patrol?

A   You mean at school?

Q   At school or outside of school.

A   No, not that I know of, no.

Q   Did you like Randy?

A   Yeah.

Q   Did he have a reputation as sort of being a good guy?

THE WITNESS: Well, he wasn't like in with my crowd so I don't really know. I knew he wasn't a guy that messes around and does a lot of wierd stuff, that's just from knowing him, but he had no reputation with any of my friends that I know.

Q   ⬛⬛⬛⬛⬛ For instance, he had never been in trouble with the law that you're aware of?

A   Not that I'm aware of, no.

Q   Have you ever known him to get into fights with anyone?

39

1   A   No.

2   Q   Had he ever been in an auto accident that you were

3 aware of?

4   A   Not that I'm aware of.

5   Q   Had you ever heard he was in an auto accident?

6   ███████████████████████████████████████

7   THE WITNESS: No, I don't remember him being in one.

8   Q   ███████████ Did Randy ever work that you're aware

9 of?

10   A   He worked at -- I think it was Army Surplus Store up

11 the street from us.

12   Q   Was that at the time of the accident he worked there?

13   A   No. I don't think he worked there.

14   Q   About how long did he work at this Army Surplus Store?

15   A   I don't know. I just know he worked there.

16   Q   Do you know what he did there?

17   A   No.

18   Q   Did you ever see him at work?

19   A   No.

20   Q   Did you ever talk to him about the job?

21   A   No.

22   Q   Do you know why he called you that morning and asked

23 you if you wanted to go out?

24   A   Do you mean do I know then or now?

25   Q   Do you know now?

26   A   Yes, because he needed an even distribution of

27 weight because four in the plane is a lot better than three.

28   Q   He didn't tell you that when he called you up?

40

    A   He said I don't want to have an empty seat so I
thought that he meant one next to him. I thought it was going
to be me and him and when he picked me up I knew what he meant
so I said that's okay.

    Q   At the time he picked you up, do you know what
experience Randy had as a pilot?

    A   His mom -- because my mom and his mom, you know, were
good friends, I knew he was real safe and he, you know, it was
his favorite thing and he really wanted to be safe, I knew he
had been safe, I'd see it go over the house every once in a while,
he'd fly over the house and she'd tell us he'd fly over, that's
all I knew about the flying.

    Q   Do you know how many hours he had logged as a flier or
pilot?

    A   No.

    Q   Do you know if he was rated to be able to fly a plane
on instruments?

    A   I don't know.

    Q   Did you ever see his flight plan he filed at El Monte?

    A   No.

    Q   Do you know if he filed a flight plan with anybody
at Apple Valley before he took off?

    A   He was at the desk for a couple minutes. He might
have. I don't know what he did. I was just standing there. I
went outside and looked around for a little while so he could have.

    Q   You don't know one way or the other?

    A   No.

    Q   Why do you think the accident happened?

65

41

1 ██

2   THE WITNESS: We just got in a storm. I don't know

3 how we got into it. I don't know if it was because Randy knew

4 it was coming and wanted to get back before a certain time and

5 took a chance or maybe the storm moved in too soon. I don't know

6 why. I've never -- people have always asked me and I've never

7 said why because I don't know.

8   Q   ████████████ Do you know if Randy was worried about

9 the weather before he took off?

10   A   Now I do. ████████████████████████████

11 ████████████ I remember he called someone on the pay phone and

12 tried to call him back for something, I guess they were busy,

13 but I think it was the weather he called, but I'm not sure. I

14 know he called somebody on the phone.

15 ██

16 ████████████████

17 ████████████

18 ██

19 ██

20 ████████

21 ████████████████████████████████

22 ██

23 ██

24   Q   Did you ever know Randy to take any drugs of any sort?

25   A   No.

26   Q   Ever known him to smoke marijuana?

27   A   No.

28   Q   Ever known him to drink alcoholic beverages?

1   A   No, but I wasn't a close friend, but from what I know

2   he wouldn't.

3   Q   At the time the Rescue Squad got there, you were the

4   only one in the plane alive?

5   A   No. When they first got there, Randy was still

6   breathing.

EXAMINATION

Q

I'm going to ask you some questions. Going back to when you were
at the Apple Valley Inn and waiting for transportation to take
you back to the airport, can you give us an idea how long you
had to wait for the transportation?

    A   Well, it wasn't right away, because I remember he had
to go to the telephone or somethint in the lobby so I just went
outside, I looked around, they had some kind of tennis court, I
remember I looked around there and maybe 10 minutes, they called
and told me to -- told him to come back and said they were were
going so they were pretty quick.

1 Q   Would it be accurate to say you left the restaurant

2 and walked into the hotel lobby part of the time, you walked out

3 the front door --

4 A   I went out the back door.

5 Q   Toward the swimming pool?

6 A   I don't know where the swimming pool is. I do know

7 where the tennis courts were.

8 Q   So, you went out there waiting on the transportation

9 A   Yes.

10 Q   Somebody else made arrangements for transportation

11 from the Inn to the airport?

12 A   Yes, they must have because I didn't.

13 Q   You don't know who it was?

14 A   No.

15 Q   When you walked outside, were you alone?

16 A   Yeah, David looked out -- I mean, he opened the door

17 to look out and see I was out there and then he shut it.

18 Q   Was the ride to the Apple Valley Inn in the same

19 vehicle you road back to the Airport in?

20 A   You mean the exact same one?

21 Q   Yes.

22 A   I don't know. They might have more than one kind of

23 van looked the same.

24 Q   Both vans?

25 A   Yeah.

26 Q   When you four rode from the Apple Valley Inn back to

27 the airport, was there anybody else in the van besides the driver

28 and the four of you?

68

4

1   A   No.

2   Q   Did you get back in the van to go back to the airport

3 in front of the Inn, the opposite door from the tennis courts?

4   A   Yes.

5   Q   Did you notice whether or not there were any other

6 people waiting for a ride back to the airport at that time?

7   A   I don't know if there was.

8   Q   Did you ever notice one way or the other whether

9 there were people waiting for a ride back to the airport?

10   A   I never looked. I never looked.

11   Q   When you got back to the airport, if I understood

12 your testimony correctly, all four of you went into the terminal

13 building.

14   A   Not when we got back from the Inn.

15   Q   Did the driver take you directly to the airplane or --

16   A   He drove pretty close to it. I don't know, Randy

17 might have got out, but I think he talked to the guy while we

18 went to the plane. He might have been giving him a tip or

19 something.

20   Q   He dropped you --

21   A   He went back --

22   Q   Then the three of you walked over to the plane --

23   A   Yes.

24   Q   And the three of you got in the airplane?

25   A   Yes.

26   Q   Was the canopy open or closed before you got there?

27   A   I don't know. I was looking at all the planes, Some-

28 body might have opened it, when I got in it it was open.

1   Q   When the three of you were waiting for Randy, was the

2   canopy open or closed?

3   A   I think it was open, but David might have closed it

4   because it was getting windy because it was cold.

5   Q   So, while you were waiting probably David closed the

6   canopy?

7   A   I'm not sure if it was closed.

8   Q   You said that Randy used a pay telephone to make a

9   call.

10   A   Yes.

11   Q   Was that at the airport or at the Inn?

12   A   At the Inn.

13   Q   Do you know who he was trying to call?

14   A   No.

15   Q   He indicated he made a call and was waiting for a

16   return call?

17   A   Yes.

18   Q   Was that before or after --

19   A   After --

20   Q   Was that during the period of time when you were

21   outside?

22   A   That was before I went outside.

23   Q   Would it be accurate to say you waited around inside,

24   Randy made a phone call, waited to be called back and then some

25   conversation took place and you walked outside?

26   A   Yes.

27   Q   You don't know who he called and who he was waiting

28   to get a return call from?

1   A   No.

2   Q   Did you notice whether or not there were any phone

3 calls made at the airport itself?

4   A   After we came back from the Inn?

5   Q   Either after or before.

6   A   Well, when we came from the plane, first got there,

7 I went and sat down with David and the girl on like a couch and

8 Randy went up to the counter.

9   Q   Inside the terminal building?

10   A   Yes. Right near the couch there was sort of an open

11 window or a counter where Randy walked over, the couch is like

12 a little "C" and he walked over a little ways over there.

13   Q   He walked over to the counter and talked with some-

14 body?

15   A   Yes.

16   Q   Did he make any phone calls there?

17   A   I wasn't watching. I was talking to David and the

18 girl.

19   Q   Do you remember any other phone calls made at or

20 near the airport?

21   A   I don't remember any.

22   Q   Now, when you took off from El Monte Airport you

23 became aware the airplane was climbing by looking out the

24 window and seeing it --

25   A   Yes.

26   Q   When you descended into the Apple Valley Airport, were

27 you able to see or tell you were going down by seeing the ground

28 coming up?

1   A   Yes.

2   Q   When you took off from Apple Valley, you were aware

3 you were climbing?

4   A   Yes.

5   Q   I think you told us just before the crash you heard

6 some conversation between Randy and David and the airplane started

7 descending. Is that correct?

8   A   Do you mean just directly --

9   Q   Just before the crash, you heard Randy and David --

10   A   He was trying to pull up but he couldn't.

11   Q   But, before that, the airplane had descended.

12   A   Yes.

13   Q   That was just moments before.

14   A   No, that was a little time before that.

15   Q   When the airplane started descending, was it before

16 or after Randy had talked on the radio and used the word emergency?

17   A   I think it was after.

18   Q   So, would it be accurate to say you had no awareness

19 of the airplane descending until after Randy used the word

20 emergency on the radio?

21   A   It might have been descending and he realized how

22 much it was, that's why he might have said something about it.

23 I can't say.

24   Q   At the time he declared the emergency, you were aware

25 there were clouds built up all around the airplane?

26   A   Yes.

27   Q   Did you hear the words used to make a turn, 180 degree

28 turn?

A   Yes.

Q   Do you remember somebody saying that --

A   I don't know if that were the exact words, but they mentioned something about a turn, go back --

Q   But you had the impression something was said about making a turn to go back.

A   Yes.

Q   You heard a response --

A   Not -- I remember telling him -- I don't remember him --

Q   Do you remember a response or anything that he could not turn or make a 180 degree turn or he couldn't turn around?

A   I remember something, but I don't know if that's what he said. I don't know exactly. I can't be sure. I don't remember what he said.

Q   But you do have a recollectionof somebody saying something about turning around to go back?

A   I don't know if they said go back, they said some kind of degree turn.

Q   You don't know whether or not the airplane made a turn?

A   No.

Q   Was that on the radio you heard ir ot was it a conversation between David and Randy?

A   On the radio.

Q   Did you hear any conversation between David and Randy about turning around and trying to go back?

A   No.

49

Q   You don't remember one way or the other?

A   No.

EXAMINATION

Q   ██████████████████████████████████ You just
commented that just before the crash David and -- David was
telling Randy to pull up and then you said he couldn't. What
did you mean by that, that he couldn't?

A   Because he was telling him, pull back, I can't, I
can't, I can't, I guess because of the weight and I guess icing
up, he couldn't make it, he was telling him to but he kept saying
I can't, I can't, just real loud and yelling at each other, kind
of --

50

1

2   Q   You don't remember him saying anything specific other

3   than he couldn't do it?

4   A   No.

5   Q   And you'ever never had any pilot training, have you,

6   Jim?

7   A   No.

8   Q   Do you know very much about airplanes?

9   A   No.

10   Q   So, any statements you might have just made about

11   why he couldn't would have been pure speculation and a guess on

12   your part, wouldn't it?

13   A   Yes.

14

15

16

17

18

19

20

21

22

23

24

25   * * * * * * * *

26   / / / /

27   / / / /

28

PTSD

Now (2024), I look back and can't believe that I survived such a tragic accident and dire situation. As of 2024, I have been teaching for thirty-five years and coaching for forty years. I share my story with my players and students when I feel the timing is right. The same question has been asked many times in the past: "Do you have Post-Traumatic Stress Disorder?" (also known as PTSD)

And you know what? I don't think so. I dealt with the accident and my injuries as a part of my life and something I needed to overcome to be successful in life. I do have a view as to why I was a survivor, and nothing that has happened in my life has swayed me away from this belief or revelation. More on my beliefs later. I do tell my students that I have dreams about plane crashes, but these crashes appear far off in the distance and are always big plane crashes, and I am never involved in the actual crash. I don't know if this is symbolic at all, but I will never know if these dreams are related to my ordeal or not.

There have been so many unreal things that have occurred in my life, but at the time these moments were occurring, they didn't seem unreal at all. Later, after looking back, I realized that they were unreal and all had some connection to me surviving my plane crash.

Bike Ride to San Diego

One of my favorite rides of all time was when I was about to graduate from Long Beach State. One of my classes was an exercise physiology class with an emphasis on active fitness, where our "final exam" was to ride our bikes from Long Beach to San Diego!

It was about one hundred miles! I have actually done this ride numerous times in my life. On one particular ride, the students in this class had to figure out how we would get home after the one-hundred-mile ride to San Diego. Nobody was planning on riding home after riding there. So my buddy, Brad, said he would drive my truck to San Diego, stay at our group's hotel, and bring back a couple of bikes with him, including mine. When we arrived in San Diego, all the riders, drivers, family members, and friends met at the pool area of the hotel and had a big BBQ and party, celebrating our accomplishment! One of the female leaders of our group was having a great time at the celebration.

She was a longtime staff member at Long Beach State and was really into fitness. She had to be in her mid- to late fifties. Someone noticed that she was becoming quite cozy with one of the partygoers. We all thought, *Good for her.* Of course, it was twentysomething Brad! Good for him!

Aussie: Oy, Oy, Oy!

Here is, maybe, the most unreal adventure that has happened in my life. I can't believe I had the opportunity to do what I am about to describe.

I started my coaching career at University High School in Irvine in 1985. I coached both baseball and basketball from the mid-1980s until the late 1980s. I found out later that Will Ferrell played baseball there in 1985. Wow! There will be more about him and my coaching at University High School later.

While I was in my second or third season as the assistant varsity baseball coach at "Uni," I started noticing this well-dressed gentleman at most of our home games. He just stood up on the hill overlooking our baseball stadium, would always come down after the game, and said hello to me. I figured he was just someone's parent or uncle there to watch one of our players. Finally, he came up after a game, gave me a business card, and announced that he was the owner of a company that was going to select and send local Southern California (mainly from Orange County) baseball players all over the world to play some baseball, spread goodwill, and create relationships between Americans and numerous other countries. I asked him why he introduced himself to me. He said that he had been checking around, and numerous parents, teachers, and coaches had recommended me as someone who could handle the assignment. I was single, substitute teaching (thus free in the summer to travel), young (twenty-five years old), and knew how to coach baseball.

He told me that the plan was to be gone for almost a month in July or August and initially visit New Zealand and Australia, where baseball was a growing sport at the time. He also told me that at the end of each trip, we would stop for a little vacation at resorts located between Australia and California in the Pacific Ocean. My first question was, "What is this going to cost me?" Amazingly, he said I would have to pay for NOTHING, and they would actually pay me! I couldn't believe that this was for real…but it was! So I embarked on helping the company put together a USA travel baseball team from high schools all around Orange County. Before we knew it, we had fifteen players all signed up and raring to go.

We practiced a few times, had numerous meetings with the company owners and parents, and I had to have meetings with the owner, as I was kind of an administrator on the trip. I ended up experiencing this amazing journey for three summers!

The owner explained the itinerary to me the first year.

- Spend sixteen to seventeen hours to fly to New Zealand.
- Spend four days in Auckland, New Zealand.
- Fly to Sydney, Australia.
- Spend two to three days in Sydney.
- Take a train up the coast of the state of New South Wales and stay for a week with host families in a preselected city.
- After spending a week in these preselected cities, we moved on and traveled up the coast to another group of host families in another city. We spent another week being "billeted out" with our new host families.
- Then we got to have a little four-day vacation on our way back to California. I asked the owner of the company where we were going to vacation. He told me to pick an island I would like to visit! So in my three years, I (and my teams) vacationed in the

tropical paradises of (1) Fiji, (2) Tahiti, and (3) Hawaii. Unreal!

In my few years of being the head coach and coordinator of this baseball traveling exchange group, every year we would begin by visiting Auckland, New Zealand. It turned out that for my entire life, my name, "Serven," was not my father's original last name. He was adopted by his stepfather when he was very young. I even did a family tree autobiography in middle school on the name "Serven." My father eventually informed me that his "real" last name was "Peterson." I also found out that his mother, my "Nana," was born and raised in…Auckland, New Zealand!

I had this information before my journeys and thus explored Auckland with this knowledge, which gave me a greater appreciation and interest in all I learned about my ancestor's birthplace.

While in New Zealand, my team and I went sightseeing and visited a city called Rotorua, known for its rejuvenating hot mud springs. We took a mud bath. Years later, I watched the scene from the remake of Chevy Chase's movie *Vacation* and enjoyed their "mud bath" scene. We went to professional rugby games and visited the sidelines. After one game, we were given a rugby tutorial by numerous players. We learned about and played outdoor and indoor cricket. We visited museums and got to participate in a sheepshearing competition. We ate New Zealand food and drank their drinks. We went to Maori museums (Maoris are the indigenous people of New Zealand). We went to a Maori celebration, which was very similar to a Hawaiian Luau. We even went to the dog races.

After leaving New Zealand, we always flew into Sydney, Australia. We would always stay at a nice hotel in the middle of Sydney. We spent numerous days exploring and learning about that great city. We visited the Opera House. We went on the Sydney Harbor Bridge. We visited many beaches, including our favorite—Bondi Beach. We went to an Australian Rules Football game and got to meet the players. We even visited King's Cross (Sydney's red-light district).

Each year after leaving Sydney, we got on the train and went north up the coast of that state, New South Wales. We stayed in fantastic, safe, and beautiful cities like Port Macquarie, Gosford, Coffs Harbor, and the country music capital of Australia, Tamworth. Other years, we stayed in the state of Queensland, in cities like Surfers Paradise and Brisbane. We played numerous baseball games against local baseball clubs. One of the select cities had a carnival at a church for our "USA" baseball team. We were in the newspaper and interviewed by local television stations. We spoke at schools. We visited museums. We went to Aboriginal celebrations. We went surfing. We played more rugby. We went snorkeling at the Great Barrier Reef. We played basketball. We visited an "outhouse" museum. We went to alligator farms. We rode horses. We went to casinos. We went to OTB (off-track betting) sites. We had so much fun. Unreal.

In Tamworth, the host families had a mini-carnival going on. As our bus pulled into town, we were thrilled to find out the carnival was…for us. And guess who the guest speaker was…ME! Was I surprised? At the carnival, I met my host—the mayor of the city. He had a nice family with a very nice wife and an eighteen-year-old daughter at the house. My assistant coach, Brad, admonished me not to flirt with her, or we could have (kiddingly) an "international incident." I assured him that I was way too professional for that. We enjoyed the carnival, and at the end of the night, we were all loading up and moving on to our host families' homes when we realized that we couldn't find Brad anywhere. We looked around, and eventually he came walking from behind a building, unaware that we were all looking for him. To everyone's surprise (actually, not to mine), he was strolling along, holding hands with…the mayor's daughter.

All our four-day "vacations" in the tropical locales were wonderful. Fiji, Tahiti, and Hawaii were all amazing places to visit. We did make sure to have our "USA" baseball team visit Pearl Harbor when we were in Hawaii.

Babe Dahlgren

After accepting the offered job of sophomore basketball coach at University High School, I noticed during our games that an older gentleman would come to my games and observe. I thought he was just a supporter of the school's sports teams. It turned out that he was…a big supporter and a member of the school's sports booster club. After our season was over, we had a conversation, and he introduced himself as a sports booster. He wanted to know if I was interested in coaching baseball at the school. So the head coach contacted me, and I happily accepted the job as the varsity assistant baseball coach. I did ask the booster club member why he had come to our games and asked me to assist the varsity baseball team. He explained that his name was Babe Dahlgren, and he used to live in Arcadia (which is next to my hometown of Temple City). He owned the local bowling alley/indoor baseball batting cage that our teams used to train at. He said he knew about my plane crash, had followed my career at Temple City High School in basketball and baseball, and thought that I would be a perfect fit for the baseball program. It happened that his grandson, Matt Dahlgren, was a catcher on the varsity team.

Over the next year, I had numerous conversations with Mr. Dahlgen. He would talk about guys named George and Lou, who used to be old teammates of his during his baseball career. Remember that this was in the 1980s, before the widespread advent of computers. Years after my coaching stint at University High School ended, I happened to be reading a story about the New York Yankees. It was telling the story of Lou Gehrig, what he went through, and how his career ended when he was afflicted with an ACL, which is now widely known as "Lou Gehrig's Disease." The story goes that Lou went to his manager in-between games of a doubleheader and said he couldn't physically play the next game, and as it turned out, he never played again. This is after playing 2,130 games consecutively!

The manager looked down the bench and had to ask the only other first baseman he had if he was ready to play. That player was a youngster named Babe Dahlgren. It dawned on me that when Mr. Dahlgren was speaking of Lou, he was talking about Lou Gehrig. And when he spoke of George, he was speaking of George Herman "Babe" Ruth! Babe Dahlgren's grandson, Matt Dahlgren, was a great young man who went on to play college baseball and write a book about his grandpa and his grandpa's long professional career, which unfortunately was marred by a rumor of marijuana use. The book is called *Rumor in Town: A Grandson's Promise to Right a Wrong*, by Matt Dahlgren.

William and Patrick

While coaching at University High School, I had a player named Patrick. He was a very talented sophomore basketball player. During the season, he mentioned that his brother had played at "Uni" and was now attending USC. Patrick said his brother came home on some weekends and would like to possibly help at practices with us on weekends. I checked with the head varsity coach if it was okay, and he said that his brother had played there and was a great guy and that it was okay with him. This sophomore, Patrick, was soon called up to varsity, but in the meantime, his brother, William, helped out on Saturdays and attended some Friday games. I would always say that he was my "assistant." The family's last name was Ferrell, and William was Will Ferrell—the actor. I was also invited to a concert of some sort to watch their dad, Lee Ferrell, play the keyboard for some band. It turned out that the band was the Righteous Brothers, and I sat in the front row watching Bill Medley belt out his hits.

First Coaching Job

In my early twenties, I lived with my brother in Newport Beach. He was the head high school basketball coach at Newport Harbor High School and encouraged me to become a high school basketball coach too. I was already refereeing high school basketball games (stories related to refereeing will come later), so the thought of coaching was very intriguing to me. So I had an interview at University High School in Irvine. I was interviewed by the head coach and a couple of his assistants. I thought the interview went well until the head coach called me a couple of days later and said they were not going to hire me. I asked him why and what I could have done better, and he told me that one of his assistants had previously been a head coach at a school in the San Gabriel Valley and had remembered me as a player at Temple City High School. The assistant said he remembered me as a cocky, arrogant player with an atrocious attitude! I couldn't believe it! I told the coach I was a hardworking player who never showed arrogance or cockiness. I couldn't understand where he got that impression. So the head coach called his assistant to get clarification. After a short discussion with the assistant, the truth was revealed—the assistant coach had me confused with my brother, who fit the description to a tee. The assistant said he remembered my plane crash and realized he had confused me with my brother. My two brothers and I all played varsity basketball at TCHS. It was a classic case of mistaken identity. Today, I still contemplate that my brother almost sabotaged my forty-year coaching career. I learned to never burn bridges because you never know what the future holds.

Love Story

Here's a good time to share my love story with my wife, Laura. This is from a story in the *LA Times* written by me.

"Why do you think you were the only survivor?" That's a question I've heard many times over the years since I was in an airplane that crashed, killing everyone else aboard.

I was a typical fifteen-year-old growing up in the San Gabriel Valley. A friend and neighbor who had a pilot's license invited me and two others for a ride one day—February 12, 1978. We flew out of El Monte Airport to Apple Valley, had lunch, and were on the way back when we hit a storm. The pilot became disoriented and began flying too low. He was only eighteen and hadn't had much experience flying in weather like that. We clipped a tree and came crashing into a snowbank west of the Cajon Pass. It was nearly a day of frigid cold *before I was rescued*. I was in intensive care for weeks with severe frostbite, a fractured leg, and hip injuries. The doctors discussed with my parents the possibility of amputations.

I didn't know much about life yet, and I sure didn't have any idea why I'd been the sole survivor. I worked hard to overcome my injuries and ended up being a pretty good baseball and basketball player at Temple City High School. So after a short three years, I was eighteen and a baseball player at a summer team party to which one of my teammates had brought his girlfriend. And *she* brought a seventeen-year-old friend with her, Laura.

I thought Laura was the sweetest, nicest, and most beautiful girl I had ever seen. We became friends. She happened to work at a sunglasses store at the Santa Anita Mall. So that may explain why I visited the mall more and more that summer. We eventually had a few dates. On one date, we went to a concert in LA to see John Waite and Scandal. They became my favorite musical acts, and I'm sure it had to do with the memories of being with Laura that night.

By the fall of that year, real life had intruded. We were both busy with life after high school. She began working and was living at home in Arcadia. I moved about an hour away to Huntington Beach. I had just started classes at Cal State Long Beach and had a night job at a gym in Seal Beach. Smartphones and email weren't around yet. There was never a breakup. We just kind of drifted apart.

After college graduation, I began teaching and coaching basketball and baseball at a high school in Irvine, where I met the co-owner and director of an international sports exchange program. They arranged to send baseball players all over the world on adventures related to their sport. I was invited to coach a group of young players and accompany them to Australia and New Zealand for more coaching and tournaments. I couldn't believe my luck. It didn't even sound real. Needless to say, I joined up and had some of the greatest adventures you could imagine. I was scared to death to fly. But I figured that if I was going to go anywhere in the world, I'd have to fly. (It helped that there were free alcoholic beverages on international flights in those days.) It was worth it, though.

I visited Australia, New Zealand, and numerous islands in the Pacific, including Tahiti, Fiji, and Hawaii.

It all led to a new opportunity for adventure. I was invited by a local baseball club in Australia to return Down Under and run its growing baseball organization for a stint. All expenses were paid. I was only substitute teaching at the time, with no real connections or commitments, so I was all in. I bought my plane ticket, told my landlord that I would be leaving, and made arrangements for my parents to take care of my two Siberian huskies, Thor and Zeus, while I was gone.

One of my buddies happened to mention that he had run into someone who said she knew me and had dated me briefly and wanted to get in touch with me. He couldn't remember her name, though.

My reaction? "Who cares! I'm going to Australia!"

I ran into him again a few weeks later. He said the same woman had asked about me again. He began searching his memory for her name. I told him I still didn't care and that I'd never met anyone I'd had special feelings for or really cared that much about. Well, except for that one girl back in high school.

"Laura!" he said, finally remembering. "Her name was Laura."

My jaw dropped.

I called my mom and asked her if she still had our old phone book in the kitchen. She did. I asked her to look under the Ks for Laura's last name. Nothing there. Then she looked under the Ls, and she recited the number she'd written there so many years ago under "Laura."

Would the number still work? Did she still live there at her mom's house? Amazingly, she answered. We talked and talked and talked. I asked if I could visit her that evening. I gladly made the hour-plus drive from Huntington Beach to Arcadia. I took my huskies with me for moral support. I stayed until 10:00 p.m., just talking on her porch, until it was finally time to drive back to the beach.

I couldn't sleep that night. So I drove back to Arcadia before dawn the next morning, left flowers on her porch, and then drove back to Huntington Beach yet again for my substitute teaching job that day.

Within a week, I had canceled my flight to Australia.

Within five months, on Valentine's Day weekend (and the anniversary date of my plane crash), I paid to have an airplane fly over Huntington Beach towing a banner that said, "Laura, will you marry me? Love, Jim."

You see, I finally had my answer to why I survived.

Letters to My Kids

It is important to know that the greatest joy in my life is my family. I love my wife and my three kids so much.

Jonathan is my oldest. Brian is my middle child, and Kristina is my youngest. When they turned eighteen (or near their high school graduation time), I decided to write them a letter, expressing how I felt about having the privilege to raise them and watch them grow into incredible young adults. Here are those letters.

Jonathan,

Happy Birthday, Jonathan! I can't believe you are eighteen. September 3, 1993, was one of the greatest days of my life. You were a beautiful baby boy. I was so happy that your mom and I had a son. We had decided that when we got married, we should live in a safe, family-friendly place away from the big cities so we could concentrate on raising our family. La Quinta and Palm Desert have been wonderful places to raise a family. You are my joy in life. I often contemplate what life is all about, why we are here on earth, and sometimes wonder why I lived through my plane crash and how I ended up with such a great wife (who is also the best mom ever) and family. In my heart, I know why—so I could be your father. Nothing in life has given me more joy than raising you, Brian, and Kristina. I have had many adventures in life, but getting the chance to raise you guys has been the absolutely most precious and rewarding experience I can ever imagine.

As I look at you as you turn eighteen, I see a very handsome, confident, strong (physically and emotionally), intelligent, focused, funny, and wonderful young man. I couldn't be prouder!

I have thoroughly enjoyed watching you embrace a healthy lifestyle with all of your working out and eating healthy. Thank you for leading Brian down the same path. This should be a lifelong passion and will help you stay in good health for a lifetime.

Also, watching you and Brian (and hopefully Kristina) evolve into truly elite athletes brings absolute joy to my heart. Watching you compete is an incredible experience, which I will always cherish.

Finally, seeing you overcome your back problems is such a relief and makes me very happy (as I'm sure it does for you too).

We have had so many memories as a family and as father and son that they are mind-boggling. I want to reminisce a little for you (and me!). Some of these you may not even remember.

– Amusement park trips and other fun events: Disneyland, Knotts

Berry Farm, Sea World, San Diego Wild Animal Park, San Diego Zoo, the Living Desert, Soak City, Legoland, The Date Festival, Pomona and Orange County Fair, Mission Beach (Belmont) Park, The Harlem Globetrotters, The Long Beach Aquarium, Universal Studios (isn't that "super"?), Medieval Times after a Clippers game, riding wave runners in the bay— every trip was very special.

- Family vacations: Hawaii, San Diego, Newport Beach, Las Vegas, Big Bear, the Point in Phoenix, Arizona, Colorado, Catalina Island, Niagara Falls, Flagstaff, Tarrytown, Sleepy Hollow, Cleveland, Utah, Steamboat Springs, Venice Beach, and the all-time Champion Trip—our drive to Cooperstown, NY.
- All of our "Rec" teams: youth baseball in PD and LQ, the Dodgers in Temple City, YMCA

basketball, soccer, flag football, golf camp practices, games, and team parties.

— Angel games (2002 World Series Championship Game), Dodger games, Padre games, Rockies games, and Yankee games.

— Our trip to Omaha, Nebraska—another fun family drive!

— Visiting Hall of Fames: Cooperstown (baseball) and Springfield, Massachusetts (basketball).

— Our year in Temple City—Little League, the Boat, Taco Lita, basketball in the alley, Wiffle ball in the backyard, etc.

— All of our trips with the girls basketball teams, especially Hawaii, and sitting on the bench helping me coach.

— All of our times with the Clippers! (Y'all, win?)—games, tournaments, and practices.

— All of our times with the Storm (and Titans, Patriots, and

Sluggers): games, tournaments, practices, and parties!

- All of our trips with high school basketball teams: Lake Tahoe, Monterrey, Big Bear, Del Mar, Huntington Beach, and Irvine.
- Your incredible CIF Championship season with the varsity baseball team at PDHS.
- All of the games, tournaments, practices, camps, team dinners, etc. with the Aztecs basketball teams.
- All the places we visited on all our trips: Busch Stadium, Fenway Park, Wrigley Field, Soldier Field, Salem Witch Museum, Cheers, the NY Subway, Downtown New York City, the Twin Towers, the Statue of Liberty, and the Little League World Series.
- The incredible experiences of our Cooperstown trips—Home Run Champion!, dorms, games, hanging out, etc. I could write an entire paper on those trips.

—   All your Branch West events, camps, and showcases.

Then there were all the things we did at home—rocking you as a baby in my arms as we listen to good night music; wrestling in the living room; doing "puncha puncha;" playing on the Slip 'N Slide in the backyard; basketball in the front yard; Wiffle ball games; pitching in the driveway; playing catch with baseballs and footballs; learning how to slide; swimming in our pools; going to all your events at Tot Stop, Gerald Ford, Cloverly, and Palm Desert Middle School and PDHS; going to the dollar movies (and you and your blanket; your first movie was *Pocahontas*); bowling; bike rides; coming to the gym on Sundays while all the guys played hoops; playing Scotty full court in our garage; driving our cars while on my lap; going in the baby jogger (at six months old); holding you tight as they stitched up your cut under your eye when you were three; kicking the soccer ball; doing homework; playing on our swing set in the backyard; golf cart rides; going to the park; birthday parties; reading books (A Fly Went By, Snug House, Bug House—remember Dot?); watching movies and TV together (*Lion King* for at least one hundred straight days!); playing with your cats and dogs—Thor, Zeus, Rocky, Buddy, Champ, Sammy, Venus, Peanut, and Kiki; listening to country music together; barbecuing; going out to dinner—Red Robin, Islands, and all those All-Pro Pizza nights; spending time together on holidays—Christmas, Thanksgiving, and Easter (egg hunts); hanging out with all our friends and family; lifting weights together; teaching you how to ride a bike AND drive; seeing your face when you got your truck; and being involved in your college recruiting process. There are many, many, many more memories…

Being able to coach you all these years is one of the greatest gifts I could ever ask for. You are and will always be my angel. I hope you have a special Senior year and reach all of your goals in life. I will always be there for you, and I love you this much (I think you know how far I am stretching my arms). I am proud of you and hope you have a great life. I know some people who can't wait until their children move out. I can't imagine how someone with a son like you could feel that way. I have never had a son graduate and move on with his life, so I think you know this isn't easy for me. But I know you will do the right thing in life, be successful, and will have a wonderful family, just like we do.

Love,
Dad

PS: And now for your Senior Year!!!!! Wow. What a year! You had the best basketball career in the history of Palm Desert High School. You led us in so many ways (physically and in terms of leadership). Reaching the

CIF Semis and the State Tournament was amazing. Being able to watch you (and Brian) play and play together so well has really been a highlight of my life. Your baseball career has been just as amazing. We still might win CIF in baseball. Once again, being able to watch you and your brother excel is another highlight! And…then the ultimate highlight of your senior year—signing with Long Beach State!

I will have the joy of watching you for years to come, maybe even in the pros.

I have tried to give you lots of freedom this year (I hope you have noticed this). Enjoy the last month of your senior year (Prom, Graduation, and Award Ceremonies). Your mom, Kristina, and I are so proud of you. We love you.

Brian,

Happy 18th Birthday! I can't believe how fast time has gone! May

5, 1995, was one of the greatest days of my life. A beautiful baby boy with blonde hair and blue eyes was born at Desert Hospital to a very happy dad, mom, and big brother! We brought you home to our house in La Quinta and rocked you to sleep every night, listening to soothing music. You have been such a joy to raise. You were always very tough (doing somersaults on the driveway!). You have grown into a handsome, intelligent, caring, and wonderful young man! I always believed that I lived through my plane crash for a reason, and with you, Jonathan, and Kristina (and Mom), I know what the reason was! You have been a precious and wonderful son. I love you very much.

I am very proud of you. You have embraced a healthy lifestyle by working out and working hard at everything you do. You will stay healthy your entire life if you keep working out. And...you have become a true ELITE athlete. I hope it has something to do with all those practices and work we did when you were young. You are amazing. Keep working hard, and you will be in the Major Leagues!

We have had so many memories that I can't even remember them all, but I will try to recall some for you.

- All of our trips: Disneyland, Universal Studios, Sea World, Legoland, your favorite and mine—Knotts Berry Farm, Medieval Times, San Diego Mission Bay, the amusement park in San Diego, Angel games, Dodger games, Padre games, and all the hotels!
- All of our family vacations: Hawaii, San Diego, Las Vegas, Newport Beach, Big Bear, The Point in Phoenix, Arizona, Colorado (Steamboat Springs and Colorado Springs), Catalina Island, Niagara Falls, Flagstaff, Tarrytown, Sleepy Hollow, Cleveland, Utah, Venice Beach, Boston (Salem Witch Museum),

Springfield (Basketball Hall of Fame), and the ALL-TIME greatest trip—driving to Colorado, staying for a week for your tournament in Steamboat Springs, and then driving all the way to Cooperstown for Jonathan's tournament. Also, going to the Baseball Hall of Fame and then driving home through St. Louis and letting you see the Cardinal Stadium, Pujol's restaurant, and Ozzie Smith's restaurant. Also, our trip to Omaha was very fun.

− All the SPORTS: rec baseball teams, YMCA basketball, rec soccer, flag football, the Clippers, the Toros, the Little League Dodgers, the Storm (thank God I got to have you on my team for those years), team parties, PRACTICES, GAMES, and TOURNAMENTS (all the driving).

− High school basketball—you are the best defender EVER! It started with "2 minutes of Defense" and ended with "thirty-two minutes of defense." You are such a competitor who improved so much. I remember the ref in Corona Del Mar who asked you where you were going to college to play basketball. I am so thankful I got to coach you. I love you so much. We have had so many memories in basketball, trips to the beach, Mater Dei, San Diego, Big Bear, and ALL the GAMES and PRACTICES! Wow!

— High school baseball: What can I say? CIF Champion, CIF Player of the Year, and DVL MVP! You have been so fun to watch, and you have made me very proud. I hope to watch you for many, many more years. Fear the Fork.

Going on your recruiting trips will be times I always cherish. Here's a couple more places we visited: Fenway Park, Wrigley Field, Soldier Field, Cheers, Grand Central Station in the New York subway system, Downtown New York City, Ground

Zero–the Twin Towers, the Statue of Liberty, the Little League World Series, and baseball showcases (Area Codes, North-South events).

Then there were all the things we did at home—rocking you as a baby in my arms as we listen to good night music; wrestling in the living room; doing "puncha puncha;" playing on the Slip 'N Slide in the back yard; basketball in the front yard; Wiffle ball games; pitching in the driveway; playing catch with baseballs and footballs; learning how to slide; swimming in our pools; going to all your events at Tot Stop, Gerald Ford, Cloverly, and Palm Desert Middle School and PDHS; going to the dollar movies (your first movie was Power Rangers with the lights on); bowling; bike rides; driving our cars while on my lap; going in the baby jogger; kicking the soccer ball; doing homework; playing on our swing set in the back yard; golf cart rides; going to the park; birthday parties; reading books; watching movies and TV together; playing with your cats and dogs—Thor, Zeus, Rocky, Buddy, Champ, Sammy, Venus, Peanut, and Kiki; listening to country music together; barbecuing; going out to dinner—Red Robin, Islands, and all those All-Pro Pizza nights; spending time together on holidays—Christmas, Thanksgiving, and Easter (egg hunts); hanging out with all our friends and family; lifting weights together; teaching you how to ride a bike AND drive; and being involved in your college recruiting process. There are many, many, many more memories…but one of my favorites was the way you tapped your finger against your cheek, turned your head to the side, and had a wonderful happy look on your face, and…sang "God Bless America" at my basketball game!

And now my little blond-haired, blue-eyed baby is all signed with Arizona State, about to graduate, enjoyed his Proms, had an unbelievable career at Palm Desert High

School, and got to share lots of this with his big brother, who always called you "Brocken." Enjoy the final days of high school and ALL the AWARDS. Your mom, Kristina, and I are so proud of you and love you so much!

Kristina,

Happy Birthday! I can't believe you are eighteen. December 9, 2002, was one of the greatest days of my life. You were a beautiful baby girl. I was so happy that your mom and I had a beautiful girl. I get to have a daughter! We had decided when we got married to live in a safe, family-friendly place away from the big cities so we could concentrate on raising our family. La Quinta and Palm Desert have been wonderful places to raise a family. You are one of my joys in life. I often contemplate what life is all about, why we are here on earth, and sometimes wonder why I lived through my plane crash and how I ended up with such a great wife (who is also the best mom ever) and family. In my heart, I know why… So I could be your father. Nothing in life has given me more joy than raising you, Jonathan, and Brian has. I have had many adventures in life, but getting the chance to raise you guys has been the absolutely most precious and rewarding experience I can ever imagine.

As I look at you as you turn eighteen, I see a very beautiful (inside and out), confident, strong (physically and emotionally), intelligent, focused, funny, and wonderful young woman. I couldn't be prouder!

I have thoroughly enjoyed watching you embrace a healthy lifestyle with all of your working out and eating healthy. This should be a lifelong passion and will help you stay in good health for a lifetime.

Also, watching you, Jonathan, and Brian evolve into varsity-level athletes brings absolute joy to my heart. Watching you compete is an incredible experience that I will always cherish.

We have had so many memories as a family and as father and daughter that it is mind-boggling. I want to reminisce a little for you (and me!). Some of these you may not even remember...

- Amusement park trips and other fun events: Disneyland, Knotts Berry Farm, Sea World, San Diego Wild Animal Park, San Diego Zoo, the Living Desert, Soak City, Legoland, the Date Festival, Pomona and Orange County Fairs, and Mission Beach (Belmont) Park. Every trip was very special.
- Family vacations: Hawaii (and with the softball team), San Diego, Huntington Beach, Newport Beach, Las Vegas, Big Bear, the Point in Phoenix, Arizona, the Grand Canyon, Sedona, Colorado, Niagara Falls, Flagstaff, Tarrytown,

Sleepy Hollow, Cleveland, Utah, Steamboat Springs, Fort Worth/Dallas, Texas for ASU Regionals, Venice Beach, and the all-time Champion Trip—our drive to COOPERSTOWN, NY.

- Club and high school volleyball games—there were so many games…ask Grandpa.
- High school varsity basketball games—you were All-League as a sophomore.
- Having you on my varsity softball team for three years and hopefully a fourth!
- Your overcoming and working hard after your knee injury to make it back to play sports (just like me after my plane crash).
- Visiting colleges to watch your brothers.
- ALL of our Arizona State baseball trips—Scottsdale, Phoenix, Tempe, and Tucson.
- All of our "Rec" teams: youth softball in PD, club and all-stars softball, YMCA basket-

ball, soccer, all the practices, games, team parties, and shooting three-pointers in the PDHS gym.

- Baseball games: watching your brothers at Arizona State and Long Beach State and staying in so many hotels.
- Our trip to Omaha, Nebraska—another fun family drive!
- Our year in Temple City—Little League, going to the park with your mom, the Boat, Taco Lita, etc.
- All the places we visited on all our trips: Busch Stadium, Fenway Park, Wrigley Field, Soldier Field, Salem Witch Museum, Cheers, the NY Subway, Downtown New York City, the Twin Towers, the Statue of Liberty, the Little League World Series, San Luis Obispo, San Francisco, and Las Vegas.

Then there were all the things we did at home—rocking you as a baby in my arms as we listen to good night music; wrestling in the living room; doing "puncha puncha;" playing with Barbies in your room (my favorite); playing on the Slip 'N Slide in the backyard; basketball in the front yard; Wiffle ball games; pitching in the driveway; playing catch with the softball; learning how to slide (still working on it!); swimming in our pools; going to all your events at Ronald Reagan and Palm Desert Middle School and PDHS; taking karate; going to the movies— Hannah Montana, Victoria Justice's concerts, Jonas Brothers' concert in our backyard; bike rides; kicking the soccer ball; doing homework; playing in our yard; golf cart rides; going to the park; birthday parties; reading books; watching movies and TV together; playing with your cats and dogs—Thor, Zeus, Rocky, Buddy, Champ, Sammy, Venus, Peanut, and Kiki; hanging out with both Grandmas and Grandpa; listening to country music together; barbecuing;

going out to dinner—Red Robin, Islands, and all those All-Pro Pizza nights; spending time together on holidays—Christmas, Thanksgiving, and Easter (egg hunts); hanging out with all our friends and family; lifting weights together; teaching you how to ride a bike AND drive; seeing your face when you got your VW car; and the night we danced in the backyard to all the father/daughter country songs. I'm crying right now… There are many, many, many more memories…

Being able to coach you all these years is one of the greatest gifts I could ever ask for. You are and will always be my angel. I hope you have a special rest of your Senior year and reach all your goals in life. I will always be there for you, and I love you this much (I think you know how far I am stretching my arms). I am proud of you and hope you have a great life. I know some people who can't wait until their children move out. I can't imagine how someone with a daughter like you could feel that way. I have never had a daughter graduate and move on with her life, so I think you know this isn't easy for me. But I know you will do the right thing in life—be successful and will have a wonderful family, just like we do.

Love,
Dad

PS: And now for your Senior Year!!!!! What a crazy year...a pandemic... I have tried to give you lots of freedom this year (I hope you have noticed this). Your mom, Jonathan, Brian, and I are so proud of you. We love you.

Here's an update on my kids as of 2023.

Jonathan

After earning a baseball scholarship to Long Beach State University (my alma mater), he was a starting infielder for a couple of years as a LB State Dirtbag. He finished his degree and embarked on a teaching career. He currently teaches multiple subjects at his alma mater, Palm Desert High School, coaches baseball, and has coached basketball there too.

Kristina

Kristina is a student at Arizona State University and started out working on a business degree, but the lure of being involved in education pulled her in that direction. She changed her major and will now be pursuing her degree and a teaching credential so she can become an elementary school teacher.

Brian

He earned a baseball scholarship to Arizona State University and graduated with a degree in business. He was the 1st Team All-PAC 12 catcher, two years in a row, and was drafted in the fifth round of the MLB draft in 2016 by the Colorado Rockies. He made his way through the Rockies farm system, playing in A, AA, and AAA. He then made his Major-League debut on May 18, 2022.

There were two more events that were unreal to me. To be a college athlete is quite an accomplishment. I am so proud of my boys. But one weekend in their college baseball careers in 2014, in particular, stood out. I got to be in attendance at Arizona State University, as they played Long Beach State University in a baseball game, and Jonathan Serven was the third baseman for LB State, and Brian was the catcher for ASU. And…when Brian homered and was running the bases, I saw him give his brother a little look and a wink as he rounded third base.

In another poignant moment, my daughter, Kristina, decided not to play on my varsity softball team at Palm Desert High School the year after the COVID Pandemic canceled her junior year, in which she was coming into her own as a very good softball player. When she told me that she just wanted to finish her senior year as a student and move on to college, it was emotional for me, but I understood. Well, she graduated high school and moved on to attend Arizona State University. Then one day during her junior year, while she was home during a break in college, she came up to me and said, "Dad, can we go play catch and take some batting practice at Palm Desert High School?" What a moment! We did, and we had so much fun.

*****

There has been numerous events, situations, and occurrences, which are linked to my plane crash.

Pilot at Wedding

Temple City was a small town where everybody knew just about everyone else. About seven years after my plane crash, I was attending a wedding in the general area of Temple City (San Gabriel Valley) when a man approached me at the wedding and asked if I was the young man who survived the plane crash involving David Emma. I told him yes that was me. He said he was an uncle/relative/good friend of the Emmas, who were a well-known and respected large family in our area. He then told me that he was a pilot and had been flying for forty years, and that he wanted to take me up for a flight the next morning. He said it was like falling off a horse—you had to get right back on. I was adamant that I was not going to be flying with him the next day. He kiddingly told me that he'd see me in the morning. I went home after the wedding with absolutely no intention of accompanying him the next morning. Later the next evening, my mom called me and told me some startling news. Guess who just died in a plane accident? Yep, it was him.

Long Beach State Meeting

What had to be the most amazing and surreal occurrence after my plane crash was an incident that happened at Long Beach State University in 1984. I started at CSULB in 1984 after a couple of years of attending Pasadena City College. I had started to think that I wanted to be a physical therapist or a chiropractor, where I could help people with serious injuries overcome physical disabilities or other physical issues and work with them to be functional and healthy. Long Beach State is a giant university with an attendance reaching 50,000 students from all over Southern California and even the rest of California, including many students from out of state and even international students.

I enrolled in a class called "The Psychology of Being Disabled," which entailed learning how people deal with disabilities and how they can overcome the many obstacles associated with disabilities. It sounded like a perfect class for my intended career. Also, I always thought about how lucky I was not to be permanently disabled after surviving such a horrendous accident.

I remember driving to school for the Monday-only class at 7:00–10:00 p.m. I still remember where I parked—near the classroom's building. I entered the room, where there were about twenty-five students. The teacher introduced herself, and before giving us any work, she said we were going to do an icebreaker exercise, which was related to the course content. It was a great assignment.

She put us in groups of three and told us to go for a walk, get some coffee or a snack, sit, and tell your two partners the "worst thing that has ever happened to you and how you dealt with it mentally." So off we went. We stopped at one of the coffee places on campus and all looked at each other, asking who wanted to go first. I was worried and wondering if I should tell my plane crash story to two perfect strangers or just tell about some other event that was not so harrowing and intense. I felt apprehension and was somewhat nervous about opening up with such a startling story. I decided to share a different event. But the girl in our group said she wanted to go first. I was relieved, and I let her share her story first. Well, she told the other student and I that when she was younger, approximately seven years ago, her sister was in a terrible airplane crash that killed her sister and two of the other three passengers, and there was one guy who survived. Oh my God! Yes, it was Kathy Taylor's younger sister!

I sat there in disbelief. I didn't know what to do or say. I did eventually tell my group a story, but it wasn't my plane crash story. I didn't remember what I told them, but after class, I asked her if I could talk to her, and I told her that I was the sole survivor of that terrible accident. She was stunned. She asked me many questions, which were totally understandable.

Unfortunately, the stress and anxiety I felt going to that class was too much for me, and I dropped the class soon after, but just the coincidence and odds of that happening were mind-boggling!

Bishop Amat and The Wiards

After moving to Palm Desert in the early 1990s, I started coaching girls basketball at Palm Desert High School. I decided to have a summer basketball tournament and invited some teams where I was friends with their coaches. Some of the teams were from Los Angeles County, and some were from Orange County, both counties where I had previously coached. One of the teams was Bishop Amat High School from La Puente, near Los Angeles.

The head coach was an old acquaintance from my years up in Temple City. Bishop Amat was one of the local Catholic high schools where people from my area sometimes attended. I tried to meet and welcome each team on their arrival in Palm Desert.

When Bishop Amat arrived, I walked them to our gym and talked with their head coach and his assistant coach, who turned out to be his wife. While he was talking to their team, I was having a conversation with his wife, who happened to be an administrator at Bishop Amat. She asked me how I knew her husband, and I explained that over the years, coaching and being from the same area, we had crossed paths and became friends. I did tell her that back in 1978, I was in an airplane crash, and one of the passengers who unfortunately passed away was a girl who attended Bishop Amat. The look on his wife's face was unforgettable. She looked me in the eye and said that the girl who passed away was one of her friends when she attended Bishop Amat!

Well, we continued to be friends and stayed in contact. Ironically, when my family moved back up to Temple City in 2004–2005, I ended up being an assistant at Bishop Amat for the basketball season. I wasn't planning on coaching that year, but somehow and some way, I did. We ended up having one of the greatest, if not THE greatest, season in high school basketball history. Our team went 35–0 and won our League Title, the CIF Southern Section Title, and the State of California Championship. I ended up being an assistant under my friend Richard Wiard and his wife!

An Unexpected Email

Forty years after my plane crash, I received an email at my school from a Mr. Taylor. I had no idea who he was. But when I read it, I was frozen in time. I was flabbergasted. Mr. Taylor turned out to be the younger brother of Kathy Taylor, the girl who died in my plane crash. He said he googled me and saw that I was a teacher in Desert Sands Unified. That was how he got my email. He sent me a poignant email, asking me to give him a call. He said he wanted to get information about the crash that took his older sister's life. I didn't really know whether I should call him or not. But I decided to call him, and I was glad I did. He explained to me that he was just six months old when Kathy passed away. He said that by the time he was old enough to understand what happened to his sister, it was somewhat of a taboo subject in his family. And so, after many years of wondering, he thought the time was right to contact me. I called him, and we talked for a while. We talked for at least an hour. I told him everything I could, considering that I had never met his sister until that dreadful day. He was so appreciative and asked me if there was anything he could do for me. I said I didn't need anything and that it was very cathartic for me to share what I could. He asked if my students liked video games. I said of course, they all love them. He said he might have a few lying around, since he was an executive with some company called "Activision." I had no idea how big a company that was and still is.

He generously sent me numerous copies of a game called "Call of Duty." I gave them to my students. What a wonderful gesture!

Brian's Major League Debut

Something happened in 2022 that was one of the most emotional, poignant, and memorable events in my life. On Monday, May 17, 2022, in the early evening, I was outside of my house doing yard work when my wife Laura said that Brian was on the phone and wanted to talk to both of us on the speaker phone. At that point, I knew it was serious. I figured in the minute it took me to get in the house that it could be a limited number of things—getting married, having a baby, maybe he decided to give up baseball, or perhaps…the greatest news of all? We both got on the phone, and he told us, "Mom and Dad, I got called up to the Big Leagues! I am making my Major League debut tomorrow!" It was sooo emotional. We told him that we would be there! We immediately got our flight and hotel in Denver, along with Kristina and Jonathan. We flew to Denver the next day. On Brian's debut day, the MLB Channel sat with us during his first at bat and interviewed us during the at bat. On the first pitch, he hit a foul ball, and wouldn't you know it, he fouled it directly in our direction! The ball landed a few feet from Laura, and my wife, yes Brian's mother, ended up with the ball!

Unbelievable!

He ended up going 0 for 2 in his first game. But he caught well.

There was a freak snowstorm the next day. It was ninety degrees outside on his debut day and thirty something degrees the next day, and it was snowing heavily, so the next day's games were "snowed out." That meant that there was to be a doubleheader the next day, and Brian would get to start one of those games. Well, during the game he caught, he got his first MLB hit…a HOME RUN! Wow!

That was pretty amazing. But wait. His next hit…was a…HOME RUN. Double Wow! He had runners on base for both home runs, which meant they were multiple RBI home runs. It turned out that it was the FIRST TIME IN MAJOR-LEAGUE HISTORY that any player (EVER) had hit multiple RBI home runs for their first two hits (EVER).

The first night when we were being interviewed, the announcer told me that he googled us to learn any pertinent information about our family. It came up about my plane crash, and the announcer said that amazingly the radio telecast announcer for the

Rockies, Jerry Schemmel, was also a survivor of a deadly plane crash. It actually was one of the biggest air disasters ever. I ended up meeting with Jerry, and we have become friends. I had never met another plane crash survivor.

Later that season, Brian was interviewed on the top-rated radio sports show, *The Jim Rome Show*, to discuss the amazing events of his first season in the Major League. As I was listening with pride and amazement that my son was on the radio with the iconic Jim Rome, it was mentioned that Jim Rome's son played baseball in Orange County. Wouldn't you know it? At University High School in Irvine. The same school I had coached at in the 1980s!

There have been many interesting, funny, crazy, and unreal experiences since my plane crash. Here are a few.

Another Close Call

Back in the early 2000s, both my boys were REALLY into baseball. So one Thursday night, I surprised them and told them that we would be… going to…a DODGER GAME at Dodger Stadium the next day. They were so excited!

The next day at school, I was reading my favorite (and my students' all-time favorite) novel in the English class I was teaching at Palm Desert High School, *Fried Green Tomatoes at the Whistle Stop Cafe*, when I started to have a headache. As the day went on at school, my headache got worse and worse. I contemplated not taking my boys to the Dodger game but relented and decided to go. They were so excited to go. I got home from school with a terrible headache, but I figured it would go away like all headaches usually do. As we were making the drive from Palm Desert to Chavez Ravine (Dodger Stadium), my headache was getting worse. So I decided to make a detour and pick up my dad, so he could drive to the stadium from his house in

Temple City. It was only twenty-some miles from Dodger Stadium. He was up for the task and drove, and he was actually looking forward to going to the game and spending some time with his grandkids.

After we arrived, and as we were walking to our seats down the third base line, my headache was getting worse. I could barely deal with the pain. So sometime in the second or third inning, I told my dad that we needed to leave and go back to his house so I could lay down and deal with my headache. Sadly, I could barely walk. Dizzy and in tremendous pain, I had the security guards help me up the stairs toward the exit. Of course the Dodger fans, in a good-natured way, were giving me crap, with many of them telling me, "Hey, have another beer." We made it to the car, and my dad drove us back to his house in Temple City. My boys were disappointed but understood how bad I was feeling. I tried to go to sleep, but my head was hurting so bad. Because I couldn't stand it anymore, I got in my car and drove myself to the local emergency room at the local hospital! They did some tests but told me that I probably just had a bad case of the flu. They gave me some Tylenol and sent me on my way.

In the morning, I still couldn't handle the pain, so my dad volunteered to drive me and my boys back to Palm Desert. That next night, I was still in so much pain that my wife, Laura, took me to our local emergency room hospital. The hospital decided to run some tests on me and suspected that I may have something more than a "headache and the flu." They decided to do a spinal tap to check my cerebral spinal fluid. They had me curve my back, and when I was in the proper position, they stuck a very thin needle in my lower back and extracted some fluid from inside my spinal column. The technician told me not to move because if I straightened up my back, I might break the needle off in my spine. Wow. But as he was extracting the fluid, he accidentally hit a nerve in my spine, and I watched my right leg kick involuntarily. How weird. After the fluid was extracted, I was put in a room, waiting for the results of the test. At approximately 2:00 a.m., the doctor came into my room, reading my chart. I swear he was shaking his head. I said, "What is the diagnosis?"

He said after a pause, "You have MENINGITIS!" Luckily, he explained to me that I had the lesser of the two types. I had viral meningitis, not bacterial. Bacterial meningitis could be fatal! Mine was just going to take some time to go away. I had a bad headache for about a week, but I had survived a bout with meningitis!

Numbness

In the early 2000s, I was teaching my students at Palm Desert High School a unit on the Cold War. I was explaining the tension between the United States and the Soviet Union, which occurred after World War II. One of my students brought up how the movie *Rocky IV* delved into those tensions as Sylvester Stallone's Rocky fought a boxer from the Soviet Union. I told the students that there were some who gave Rocky a little credit for the thawing out of tensions with his impassioned speech at the end of the movie about how our countries should try to get along. As we were having this discussion, a student asked me why my lower lip was sagging like Rocky's did when he spoke. At this time, I looked into a mirror and noticed the left side of my mouth WAS sagging. It reminded me of Bill Murray's character, Carl Spackler, who was the greenskeeper in the classic movie *Caddyshack*. His lower lip sagged too. I also noticed that my left eye looked strange, and I couldn't blink my left eye. The left side of my face was going numb. I was scared that I was having a stroke, although the remainder of the left side of my body was fine. So I left school for the rest of that day and immediately went to my doctor, who, within ten seconds of looking at me, diagnosed me with Bell's Palsy. It turned out that Sylvester Stallone had a bad case of Bell's Palsy too. I had never heard of such a condition. It turned out that I had either pinched a facial nerve or had a virus that affected the facial nerve. Either way, it took a couple of weeks for it to go away. One major issue was that I couldn't blink my left eye, which could cause serious problems. Your eyes need to remain moist. So the doctor used some kind of medical tape (which looked to me like duct tape) and literally taped my eye shut! I told him that I felt fine and asked if I could still go to work. He said yes. I mentioned that I didn't really want to teach with a piece of duct tape over my eye. He said he was way ahead of me. He then proceeded to pull out an eye patch. So I returned to school the next day with an eye patch over my left eye. I had never heard so many pirate references! My favorite, though, was "Mr. SeRRRRven."

Arm Wrestling

Back in the mid-1980s, there was a "sport" that was becoming very popular and became somewhat of a sensation. It was arm wrestling. Being in great condition and working out all the time with all my friends gave us pause to consider signing up for the numerous arm-wrestling competitions, which were occurring almost every weekend at local sports bars and at restaurants like Chilis, the Red Onion, and others. I usually lasted a round or two, but I never even came close to winning these competitions. But we did have one friend, Kevin Jeff, who had forearms like Popeye and fingers so big, we called them "banana fingers." Also, he didn't weigh much more than 150 lbs. Because we were grouped by weight, he arm wrestled guys within his weight class. He usually defeated people who were way heavier than him. One Saturday, he entered a competition and destroyed his opponents. I just came along for the fun and to watch him, and I told everyone I was his manager. After winning the championship, instead of a trophy, he was awarded something way different than normal. He was given a part in Sylvester Stallone's new movie, *Over the Top*, which was all about arm wrestling! And I, being his "manager," was also given a small part. So off to Las Vegas! We went for three days to film the climactic scene in the movie at the Las Vegas Hilton. Getting a room for three nights was our "payment" for being in the movie. Kevin was in the movie as a contestant in the arm-wrestling scenes, and I was there right behind him, patting him on the back. That's what managers do!

Wrestling

Around 2015, I would volunteer to operate the scoreboard and clock for Palm Desert High School football games. At one game, an ex-basketball player (who was a very talented player) of mine came into the booth to say hello. He was there to watch his younger cousin. I asked how he was doing, and he said great and explained that he was going to college to become an actor. I told him of my acting career in *Over the Top*. After he was done laughing, he told me that he might be in a new movie about an Iranian boy who had to move from Iran to California because of the Iran-Iraq conflict of 1980. I told him good luck. Well, within two years, he wasn't just in the movie—he was the star of the greatest wrestling movie ever made (in my humble opinion) called *American Wrestler: The Wizard*. It was in all the theaters, including one at our local mall. Being the humble, respectful, and appreciative man he was, this star, George Kosturos, rented out the theater for Palm Desert High School's entire high school basketball program (three full teams) and attended its premiere with us. He also invited my family and me to its Hollywood premiere and allowed my family and friends to watch him walk the red carpet in Hollywood. It also starred, among others, one of the all-time great actors, Jon Voight. My daughter was hoping to meet Mr. Voight's daughter, Angelina Jolie, but she didn't attend. George said one very ironic scene in his movie was when he was trying out for different sports (which he was supposed to act like he wasn't talented in), and he had to try out for basketball. Being, in reality, very skilled, he had to use all his acting skills to look incompetent. George also made an incredible sequel to this wrestling movie. It was called *American Fighter*.

Travel Ball and Cooperstown

Back at the turn of the millennium, in the year 2000, a few friends of mine who happened to be baseball coaches noticed that we had a group of very talented seven- and eight-year-old baseball players in our growing community of La Quinta, Palm Desert, Indio, and Palm Springs. We recognized that every parent thought that their child had lots of talent in specific sports, but we knew as longtime coaches that we really did have a wealth of talent. So we started numerous travel and club baseball teams in the Coachella Valley. The talent was abundant. We had enough quality players to fill four or five high-level baseball teams. We also realized that to raise our players' levels, we would need to teach our players the correct fundamentals of baseball, but we also needed to play high-level competition, which meant lots of travel. We had a number of exceptional high-level coaches: Tim Burcham (former AAA MiLB pitcher and high school baseball coach), Mark Cresse (former Los Angeles Dodger's coach),

Brian Wiesler (former AAA MiLB pitcher and varsity high school coach), Bobb Boetto (college baseball coach), David Kato (former varsity high school baseball coach), and I would include myself (former varsity high school head baseball coach). The proof was "in the pudding," as they say. We had over thirty of our players receive college scholarships to play baseball! We even had three of our players reach the Major Leagues—Brian Serven, Brooks Kriske, and Tyson Miller. We had many others who reached the minor leagues and many who made it to AAA, including Scott Burcham and Nick Baker.

Most of our local travel teams decided to play in one special tournament, which encompassed the entire country. It was the Cooperstown Tournament. Yes, it was held in the city housing the MLB Hall of Fame. It was a great experience for all, and many of our Coachella Valley teams did exceptionally well and many reached the semifinals or the actual finals, and some won the whole thing.

One great story was when one of the teams I coached, the Palm Desert Titans, played as ten-year-olds. We were playing a team from Connecticut. Their coach explained to us that with the rain and snow in their state, they only got to play baseball for a few months of the year. He lamented that all the teams from fair-weather states (California, Texas,

Arizona, Florida, and Nevada, to name some) got to play year-round, and that made it difficult for them to compete, which was absolutely true. We defeated the Connecticut team handily, but during the last inning, an unusual event happened. The tournament we were playing in had ninety-six teams that played approximately ten games in a short week's time. So they had to have time limits. They also implemented rules to speed up the game. One rule was that if the catcher from the batting team was on base with two outs, you had to pinch run for them so they could get the catcher's gear on to save time in-between innings. So the other team's catcher walked with two outs. He was a kid who always hustled on the field. So when he walked, he sprinted to first base. He knew he was being replaced by a pinch runner, per the rules. He touched first base and immediately sprinted across the field back towards his dugout, which was directly behind third base. Our players weren't sure what was happening as he sprinted across the field, and so our pitcher ran at him and tagged him out near the pitcher's mound. The umpire kiddingly called him "out," which completely confused our team.

Well, play resumed, we retired the next hitter, and our players returned to our dugout. Still somewhat confused, they asked us what happened. One of our coaches called them together and told them that in Connecticut, since baseball had been played there since the late 1800s, they had an unusual rule that you can go straight from first to third if you run directly over the pitcher's mound, which gave the opposing pitcher the opportunity to tag you out. Our inventive coach even had a name for this ridiculously false story, the "Connecticut Cut Through." He even had a name for the technique the pitcher was supposed to use to tag out the runner, the "Piscataway Pushback." Some of our players weren't sure, but most of them knew that he was making up the whole thing! Every team at the Cooperstown Tournament was to bring an umpire with them for the week, which cut down on the huge expense of paying umpires. What a great and money-saving idea! We brought a local umpire along, who was an absolutely great guy. After the games were all over for the night, he was checking to see how we did, and the kids told him the story about the "Connecticut Cut Through" play, and he was astonished. He had never heard of such a thing. So every night after all the games were played, all ninety-six umpires would meet at a building on the grounds, go around, and discuss the day's action and any unusual situations that might have occurred. You may have guessed it—our wonderful ump told the whole group about the "Connecticut Cut Through" play, not knowing it was hogwash. The rest of the umpire group had a good laugh over that one. Our umpire came back to our team barracks with an embarrassed look on his face, and he gave us a hard time for telling him that story.

Martina the Ump

When you are involved in travel and club base-ball, you are busy every weekend and driving a lot! One weekend, we were in a tournament, about an hour and a half from Palm Desert, in a city called West Covina. Of course, they gave us an 8:00 a.m. game, which meant we had to be there at 7:00 a.m. (ish). That meant leaving at 5:00 a.m. It was beautiful weather in Palm Desert when we left, but incredibly foggy by the time we reached West Covina. We pulled up at 7:00 a.m. and walked to the field in very foggy conditions. As I was walking to the field, an umpire appeared right in front of me and said, "How are you, coach?" I said I was fine. She asked how I was doing and just kept talking to me. I have met a lot of people in my life, and she didn't look like someone I recognized. She kept walking with me and asked if I recognized her. I said I didn't. She said that I should know her. She said she knew me very well. At this point, I started to think that maybe she was someone I knew growing up, considering that West Covina was not far from my hometown of Temple City. She asked me if I remembered the umpire out in Palm Desert whom we always called if we needed a high-level ump for one of our local games or scrimmages. I said yes. The ump we always called was an excellent umpire named Martin. She looked at me in the fog and said that she was, in fact, Martin! Now she was known as Martina, the ump! Yes, she was undergoing the transition from being a man to being a woman. I was shocked but thought, *Good for her* if that was what she wanted to do. So after parting ways that morning, I shared that story with my assistant coaches. About two weeks later, we needed an ump for a game we had scheduled, so I called her to ump our game. Back in the day, people used to have songs for their ring-tones on their phones. Knowing Martin as we did and knowing what a light-hearted person he was, it was not surprising to hear Martina's ringtone when I called her. It was Aerosmith's "Dude (Looks Like a Lady)."

Rossmoor and the
Referee Jacket

Back in the mid-1980s, while I was attending Long Beach State, a friend who was going to school with me told me that I should apply for a job at his place of employment, Rossmoor Athletic Club. It was in a very nice part of Western Orange County, officially in Seal Beach but nearer Rossmoor and Los Alamitos. I became the weekend sales manager, and I was also a trainer. One of the members was a young guy who graduated from Long Beach State. His name was Greg Willard. He was an excellent basketball official in the OC. I was also officiating basketball and ended up being friends with him, and I was actually partnered with him numerous times to referee high school games. He told me he was trying to move up and wanted to become an official in the NBA. High aspirations! Amazingly, he did become an NBA referee for numerous years! While I was refereeing in Orange County, I was starting to move up the ranks. I was told that I was to be evaluated by some "higher-up" officials. My assigned partner couldn't make it, so I had to find a replacement. I couldn't find one, so I asked my friend Brad, who was an excellent official but not a certified referee in Orange County, if he would be my partner. He agreed. I told him this was important to me, so he should be professional in the official's uniform and be on time. Thankfully, he did!

So as we were conducting our pregame conference and preparing for the game, the evaluating officials came down to talk to me. They asked, "What's up with your partner?" I asked them what they meant. They told me to look at him. So I did, and then I noticed the problem. I had asked him to wear the required black jacket referees were supposed to wear into the gym. He had on a black jacket all right...but written across the back were the giant words, "BUD LIGHT." That was not an appropriate jacket to wear to a high school game. He said it was the only black jacket he had. He did take it off and referee the game with me. But while the game was going on, he stopped play numerous times (using proper mechanics, of course) and kept calling "my time" and summoning me to the scorer's table to supposedly correct an issue with the score books or the clock. But each and every time, he would feign like we were discussing a basketball issue while he was saying things to me like, "Check out that good-looking mom by the entrance." I shook my head each time and asked him to please stop doing that.

Also, while working at the gym, I met a very nice retired podiatrist who was a member. We had converted a number of racquetball courts into a basketball court, and he loved to go in there and shoot free throws. I used to rebound for him every weekend.

Well, one weekend he started shooting free throws and had quite a consecutive streak of making free throws. Before he was done, he had set a new record with a streak of…wait for it…2,750 in a row. Dr. Tom Amberry was quite a guy.

Halloween

While attending Long Beach State, my group of friends and I were invited to a Halloween party. We had no desire to spend money on costumes, but we were told that we would not be allowed into the party without one. My buddy, Keenan, said not to worry but to make sure we all had on white sweatshirts and white sweatpants before we left for the party. We were all able to come up with that outfit at no cost. We had no idea what his plan was. When we got to his apartment, he gave us all a two-foot piece of rope cut from jump ropes… We still had no idea what our costumes were. He said we would be stuffing the rope into the waistband on the back of our sweatpants. We had a couple of girls in our group of friends who were going with us. He had them put a large, white Glad trash bag over their heads. He cut holes for their heads and arms. We were also told to stuff the trash bags (which were tied at their knees) with crumbled-up newspapers. They resembled a bag puffed up with stuffing. He instructed us to try to bump into them at the party as much as possible. And then it dawned on us—we were "sperm," and they were the "eggs." I think we won "best costume" at the party!

Florida

In the late 80s, my friend, Keenan Ridgeway, and I were trying to find a fun place to go on vacation during the summer. We had a friend who lived in Tampa, Florida, and we decided to get in touch with him and see if we could stay with him for a week while enjoying the Sunshine State. Warning: Don't go to Florida in August—100-degree heat, but the worst part was the 100 percent humidity! We didn't find this out until we got there, but we tried to make the best of it.

Our friend lived in an apartment complex that was rented to lots of younger adults. There was a basketball court, a BBQ area, and a nice stream running right by the complex. So one night, while everyone was outside BBQing and just hanging out (including drinks in hand), we decided to challenge a couple of guys who were shooting around to a two-on-two basketball game. We decided to make a wager as to who would win to make the game more interesting, and it was decided that the losers had to swim across and back in the stream. The stream was about twenty yards across, so it wouldn't be too difficult if we were to lose. The crowd outside was enjoying our spirited competition, and we noticed toward the end of the game (which was very closely contested) that the people were doing an unusual movement with their hands. It was an up-and-down type of clap, and it was quickly explained to us that that was known as the "alligator chomp" sign in Florida. We didn't really think anything of it.

Toward the end of our game (it was a tie game), we upped the punishment for the loser by saying that you had to swim across...naked! We weren't worried because we were sure we would win. Unfortunately, we lost...and had to swim across. The crowd was cheering us on. We jumped in the water, undressed, and took off on an easy swim. The water was murky and muddy, but we made it to the other side quickly. Just as we reached the other side, our buddy told us to look down the edge of the stream. What we saw was terrifying—Two ALLIGATORS! We swam back so fast that I was sure we set an Olympic record. I was somewhat angry at my friend for letting us swim in the water that included alligators, but he said we were never in any danger. It was easy for him to say.

Well, the night ended. The next morning, I awoke early and noticed that my friend was fishing in the same stream. So I went outside and discussed the previous night's excitement as he was reeling in the weirdest looking fish I had ever seen. It was known as an alligator garfish. It was over a foot long and had an alligator mouth but a fish body. It was very menacing looking. I asked him if there were many of those fish in the stream, and he said that yes, there were a lot in the water. I was really mad now considering we swam across the previous night with these creatures in the water. After sharing my concerns, I asked my friend what the heck kind of bait is used to catch these garfish. To my shock and surprise, he said they use…Vienna sausages. You do the math.

Bicycle Race to Ensenada

Back in the mid-1980s, there was a bicycle event known as the Rosarito to Ensenada bike ride. A number of my friends wanted to give it a try, while another group of friends said they would drive down for the festivities, and then they would be our ride back to California. We trained for the ride, and we were really looking forward to the event. So we did the ride, and when we pulled into Ensenada, there was a big party and celebration at the finish line. People were enjoying themselves with all kinds of drinks. Unfortunately, one of the guys who drove there had been imbibing in tequila for most of the day. Many people have told me that tequila can do some bad things to you and to one's behavior. Well, at the initial celebration, we were having a good time and had discussed going to our hotel and freshening up so we would be ready to go out that night to the local landmarks, especially the well-known hot spots Hussongs and Papas & Beer.

So we decided to head over to our hotel. A large number of celebrants were crossing one of the local streets when a Mexican police officer stopped us and told us that we were jaywalking. Wow. He was going to give us all tickets, but we figured out that there may be another way out. So with a little exchange of cash, we were all released. But the officer did take our names down. Now keep in mind that I was in another country without my ID on me, so it seemed pragmatic to not tell him my correct name. My group all kind of figured that out. So (and these names come into play numerous times in our lives and adventures), the first guy who was questioned said his name was Terry Gannon. In reality, that was the name of one of the starting five on the North Carolina State Wolfpack college basketball team that had won the NCAA Championship a couple of years before. We were all avid sports fans, so we all understood what angle to take when it was our turn to give the officer our names. So the next guy said his name was Sydney Lowe (another NC St. player). My turn—I was now known as Dereck Whittenburg (the star shooter on the Wolfpack). So we were all allowed to continue our fun-filled evening, only $20.00 poorer.

Later that evening, we all went into town to join the evening party. The one friend who was drinking the tequila was kind of out of it by 8:00 p.m., but he accompanied us anyway. Well, he started to get a little (well, a lot) belligerent at the nightclubs. One thing led to another, and he kind of started a small melee. Unluckily, but expected, the police showed up and decided to load 15–20 people in what could be described as a paddy wagon. We were driven downtown to what we all believed was probably the Ensenada jail. But after taking our identification information (remember Dereck Whittenburg?) once again, it turned out to be a way for the officers to make a little cash. Whoever had $50.00 was released. How it worked was that after they read your name, you gave the officers money, and you were allowed to go on your merry way, which led us right back to the celebration at the clubs.

After enjoying ourselves and eventually ending up back at our hotel, we all wondered where the "instigator" was. Well, it turned out that he was not released and spent the night in jail. He couldn't remember his "alias" when the officers were reading back the names we had given, and he had to spend the night. When he did return the next morning, he had a black eye and some sore ribs. He thinks the other inmates beat him up for starting the original melee, but he wasn't sure because he was so intoxicated and couldn't remember…(too much tequila).

The next week, while back attending classes at Long Beach State, the Mexico story was being shared in our classes, which were held in the PE Department area. I was told during one lab class that someone wanted to meet with me in the hallway. So unsuspecting me went out in the hallway, where a rather big African American man said, "I hear you have been using my name?" Yes, it was THE Dereck Whittenburg. He had just been hired as the Assistant Men's Basketball Coach at LB State. I told him yes, I had used his name and that he was my all-time favorite player. He just laughed and gave me a hug—unreal. In a huge twist of irony, as the pickleball craze has taken over America since 2020, I play lots of pickleball with a wonderful group of picklers. Among them is the ex-NBA great Pooh Richardson, who is good buddies with "Whit," also known as Dereck Whittenburg!

Angel Game

Brad Hamilton, Keenan Ridgeway, and I decided to go to an Angel game on a Saturday night back in the day. We ended up getting very good seats near the first base dugout. We decided to go early and do what people do at sporting events—TAILGATE. So we parked under the "Big A" and had a few drinks. It was all great fun, but the game was starting, so we headed in. We discussed if there was any way we could smuggle in some "drinks" under our own sweatshirts or just roll up our sweatshirts and put the aforementioned "drinks" in the sweatshirts...so we tried. To our happy surprise, Keenan walked right in with no problems...so we headed in. Unfortunately, the security agents stopped us and asked us what we had, and after discovering our extra baggage, they asked Brad and me to accompany them to a waiting room/holding room. After questioning us, the security guard/officer (we weren't sure how official the authority figure was) asked us our birthday to verify that we were not underage. Fortunately for me, I was over twenty-one, and my release was imminent. But Brad was just under twenty-one and had trouble doing the math to match his birthdate with what would make a legal age. He fumbled with the details and gave an incorrect birth date, but quickly came up with the correct birthdate, which would make him legal, but the officer said that he was going to believe his first response because people usually tell the truth the first time they tell you something. Brad then got smart-alecky and said that if that was the case and the officer was going to believe the first thing he told him, that means that whatever Brad tells him, he should believe. So Brad said (and I quote), "I am a giant monster, and I'm going to eat you up." That didn't go over very well. The officer said that things were snowballing for Brad. Brad then said that the officer was just "a security guard and a rent-a-cop," whereas the officer produced an Anaheim police badge. I was released, and Brad was kept behind.

I was allowed to go into the game and found my friend Keenan sitting in our seats near the first base line. He was yelling at Kent Hrbek, the Twins first baseman, and eventually it became so loud and intense that they asked him to leave, so I exited with him. We waited in our truck for Brad to come out, but even after the game ended and most of the crowd had left for home, Brad still hadn't appeared. So we went and asked security where he was, and they told us that he was transported to Anaheim jail…Wow. It was too late to bail him out, and more importantly, we had had a few beers, so we just slept in our truck under the Big A sign. In the morning, we went to Anaheim jail looking for Brad, but they said he had been transported to Fullerton Courthouse to be sentenced! We hurried over to the courthouse in time to see him enter the court in handcuffs, and he had to approach the judge. The judge said that he was being charged with the felony of smuggling beers into an Angel game. Brad couldn't believe it and said, "A felony?" The judge just laughed and said of course, it was not a felony. His sentence was time served, and he wasn't allowed into Angel Stadium anymore, to which Brad sarcastically said, "But I have Iron Maiden concert tickets for next month." The judge just laughed, and Brad was released to us, whereupon we went home, and ironically, we had tickets to the next Angel game too. So of course, we attended the next day's game too.

Laker Jackets

In 1985, I was a student at Long Beach State University. I saw a flier on campus advertising Laker Season tickets for two seats at the amazing price of $5.00 a seat! So I did the math. Forty-one home games for $10.00 per game—that was $410.00 for season tickets to watch the Showtime Lakers! Now we were typical college students who didn't have much extra money. We (as the cliché goes) used to go to weddings just for the rice. We also used to get hamburgers at McDonald's cut in half! Sometimes we would just buy the piece of cheese on the order menu screen for 10 cents. But I bought the season tickets! My buddy, Brad, and I went to every home game that year. The Lakers ended up winning the NBA Championship. I explained to Brad that he would have to drive to every game because I paid for the tickets. He, amazingly, said he would split the ticket price with me. I didn't know where he was going to come up with $205, but I should have figured that there was something cooking in his head.

The first game we attended (and every game after that), we would tailgate in the parking lot with all the other Laker fans. But as we were getting ready to lock his car and go into the Forum, Brad put on his heavy-duty ski jacket. It was cold, but I didn't think he needed such a big jacket. And then I understood. He was packing beer cans in each oversized arm sleeve. Five cans in each sleeve. He became the go-to beer vendor in the arena. He sold each beer for $5.00 to other fans, making himself the cheapest vendor at the Forum. He would make $40–$50 a game! He had no trouble paying me back. And… we got to hang out with Dancing Barry!

Hi, Jack

On one of our trips to Hawaii with the high school teams (we went with the girls' basketball team at Palm Desert High School in 1995, 1997, 2000, and the 2018 softball team), we brought along a friend of my assistant coach. He was a very simple, friendly, and extremely gullible guy. So while we were flying, I told him that I knew the pilot, and, of course, he believed me. The pilot came out of the cockpit as he let his copilots fly the plane. The pilot made the rounds in the airplane, saying hi to his passengers. So I told my friend to yell at the pilot and say "Hi" from pretty far back in the plane. My friend stood up and yelled hello to the pilot. I also told him the pilot's name was Jack… So what came out of his mouth was not good for us. "Hi, Jack!" (or hijack). That didn't go over very well on an airplane. Thank God, it was Pre 9/11.

Pineapple Maze

On one of the trips to Hawaii, the coaches went on a sightseeing drive around Oahu. We went to the north shore and found the Dole Pineapple Plant Maze. It was a very large human maze in the shape of a pineapple, where people paid to weave their way through this elaborate maze and try to get out in a reasonable amount of time. It turned out that the record was seven minutes (you got some kind of pineapple prize). So we got started and soon realized that we weren't going to make seven minutes—no way in hell! We were getting frustrated and sweaty (very humid) and just wanted to get out of the maze. We were going on an hour. We finally got to the final runway, where you check your exit time to see how long it took you. So my friend came up with a fun idea. He told me to finish the final stretch and wait for him at the finish line, where many people wait for their friends to exit the maze. He told me to yell at him when he entered the final stretch that he was at six minutes and thirty seconds and to "hurry" so he could set the record. Everyone started to cheer for him, but just as he was twenty or so yards away, he "accidentally" tripped and fell. He started crawling and reaching for the ground, seemingly fighting his way to the finish. Exhausted and past the seven-minute record, he stopped just short of the finish line. The finish line crowd just cheered him on more.

Bear Poop

My friends and I used to go skiing a lot. We went locally to the San Bernardino mountains—Big Bear Mountain and Mt. Baldy—but we especially liked going to Mammoth Mountain in the Sierras. It is an eight-hour drive, but it was worth it.

Our routine would be to fill our backpacks with cans of beer and then take a lift to the top of the mountain. We would then ski "out-of-bounds" and find a secluded spot to drop off our drinks in the snow to keep them cold for our next time up the lift. Pretty smart! This way, if we met anyone, we would ask them if they wanted to get a beer. Most skiers said "sure," but they always thought we'd be skiing to the closest chalet restaurant or snack bar to get our drinks. But no, we would ski through the out-of-bounds area and stop at our hidden beer garden, away from everyone else. At this point, I must go back and explain that my friend was the only person I knew who would bring toilet paper with him while skiing. He kept it with him in his backpack, just in case. Well, one time he had to go number two, and he wasn't going to ski to a bathroom to relieve himself. He would ski out-of-bounds and go near a secluded tree. I know…kind of gross, but this one time he went to the bathroom by the trees, not too far from where we had hidden our beers. We happened to meet a couple of girls and asked them if they wanted a beer. They said sure and thus followed us out-of-bounds to our mini-brewery. Well, we went a little out of our way. It was hard to remember exactly where we left the drinks and accidentally skied near where my friend had gone number two. The girls yelled and said, "How gross! A bear must have pooped in the snow!" I looked over in amazement and embarrassment at my friend, who had the proudest look and had a big smile while nodding his head, saying, "A bear, yes, it must have been a bear!" He was as proud of himself as I had ever seen.

Car on Fire

Back in the day, Keenan, Brad and I went on a week's vacation in Florida to visit an old friend. We asked our friend to borrow his car, but he said it was a Corvette and only had two seats. Unfortunately, there were three of us. Our friend asked his neighbor if they could trade cars for a day. The neighbor had a station wagon, so we loaded up and drove the beat-up old wagon to Orlando. After a fun day at a water park, we started back. The only problem was that we really didn't know the directions. Random people told us to drive across a "land bridge" through Tampa Bay and then ask someone when we got across the bay. So we headed out across a "land bridge." We were having trouble getting the station wagon up to a good speed. Forty-five miles per hour was all we could muster. Also, we noticed a really bad smell from the car, so we just ignored it and kept on going forth. I think we rolled up the windows and just turned the radio up louder. Halfway across, we stopped to check out the car.

We did not see anything wrong. A car pulled over to help us, but both guys looked like characters out of the movie *Deliverance*, so we hopped back in and kept going. As we approached the end of the "land bridge," we knew we needed to get gas and ask for directions. There was a gas station right at the end of the bridge.

As we pulled into the gas station, the attendants were waving their arms wildly and pointing at the back of the wagon. We were on Fire! We pulled up and jumped out of the car after putting it in park, ran, and hid behind the gas station as the attendants got under our car and put out the flames with rags. As we were hiding behind the gas station, my friend ran back to the wagon. We thought he was going to help the attendants and be a hero. He came running back with our cooler, which, to his credit, was full of beers. The somewhat angry attendants put out the fire, came over to us, and asked us what we were doing behind the gas station. We said we were hiding. They said we almost blew up the entire block! They stood there and just shook their heads. It turned out that the emergency brake was stuck and never disengaged all the way from Orlando. That explained the smell, the low speed, and the fire. We decided that we were not driving it any further. So the tow truck put it up, and as we were driving away, the rear axle broke in half, which must have been from the fire. So we finally made it back to our friend's house. We had been staying with him for numerous days and were flying out the next morning. Well, in that short time, our friend's girlfriend got very upset that he spent more time with us than her, so they broke up. He missed work numerous days to hang out with us, party a little, and sometimes go somewhere with us. He stayed up late with us having a good time, and a couple of the days, he was too tired and hungover to go to work. He lost his job too. His neighbors complained that we were too loud and boisterous all week, so we heard later that he had to move, and his neighbor wouldn't give him his car back until he fixed the station wagon. That was a great week, huh?

Mom

I had a fantastic and very loving mom. She passed away in December 2011 from complications of pneumonia. The entire heartbreaking experience of losing our mother was a horrible experience. There was an incident that was very unreal and happened during this time.

Well, my brother called me in December and said that I needed to get to Arcadia Methodist Hospital (a hospital where all my brothers and I were born, and so was my wife, Laura) because our mom was really sick, and it was bad. So I left school and drove with Laura up to Arcadia. Our mom was having serious breathing difficulties. It became apparent that things were getting worse when they put her in an intensive care breathing unit. The doctor told us that she may not make it, which was very emotional and painful for my two brothers and me to hear, but especially so for my dad. So for about a week, we took turns taking care of my dad because he was like a zombie—confused, dazed, and not understanding how this could be happening. Eventually, the doctor told us that we would have to decide whether to let her pass away painfully because her condition wasn't letting her accept oxygen into her lungs or let her pass away quietly and peacefully. That was a surreal question and situation to be in! To let your only mom pass away—the woman who raised, loved, and nurtured us. It was a very painful and emotional decision for my entire family.

A day before we had to make that difficult decision, my brother and I had to do the most surreal thing—go look at caskets! The owner of the casket store was giving us a price list, and it seemed like a normal transaction, but who was prepared to do something like pick out your loving mother's casket? After that very difficult experience, my brother and I went back to the hospital to try to visit our mom in the breathing unit of intensive care. When we went up to the nurse in charge of the unit, we asked if we could see our mom. There were a few people near the nurses' stand waiting to see their family members too. One gray-haired gentleman was behind us, waiting to check on his wife. When the nurse told us that our mom wasn't doing very well and let us know they were doing some kind of treatment on her, we said we would be back in a little while. The gentleman behind us went to talk to the nurse after us.

He came away from the nurses' stand, crying heavily. We felt bad for him because we sure could understand how he felt. We watched him call his family and friends and let them know that his wife wasn't doing very well either. We heard him tell his family that she had taken a turn for the worse because the day before she was doing well. So about twenty minutes later, we left the waiting room and went back to check on our mom. The nurse said it would still be a few minutes before we could see her and asked us if we wouldn't let our dad know too. We told her our father wasn't with us at that time. She looked at us with the most incredulous face and said, "I just told your dad that your mom wasn't doing very well." We told her again that our dad hadn't been to the hospital yet that day. She said, "That gray-haired man that was with you earlier wasn't your dad?" We said no, and she looked at us and said, "Oh, my God!" She had mistakenly told the other gentleman information about OUR mom, not HIS wife. It turned out that his wife was doing very well. The nurse sprinted to the waiting room, found the man, apologized profusely, and explained the mistake to the weeping gentleman. My brother then went up to the nurse and asked her if she might have made a mistake about our mom too. Unfortunately, she had not.

Dodgers

Temple City was a great place to grow up. I was actually the "King" of Temple City in 1969 for their annual Camellia Parade and Festival. It is Temple City's version of Pasadena's Rose Parade. It wasn't far from Los Angeles and Orange County cities. We had many wonderful adventures in the area. There were mountains, beaches, amusement parks, and sporting events everywhere near us. One of our favorite family events was going to Dodger games. My mom was such a Dodger fan! Her favorite (and many other fans too) was first baseman Steve Garvey. Handsome, strong, and articulate, Garvey was a big fan favorite in the 70s and 80s. Years later, after having been living and coaching in Palm Desert, we found out that a new talented baseball player was enrolling at PDHS and would be a teammate of my two boys, Jonathan and Brian. His family was moving to Palm Desert—the Garvey's! Unfortunately, my mom passed away before she got to meet her favorite baseball player of all time. But she would have been pleased to know that her grandson, Brian, went to his Prom with Steve Garvey's daughter! Now they were just going as friends, but wasn't life full of coincidences and irony?

My Dad

I have a great father. He was a truck driver who worked very hard to support his family. He is almost 90 years old and has been through a lot. He is a Korean War Veteran who has survived cancer, COVID-19, the loss of a kidney, and a heart attack.

He is small in stature (5'7") but not in toughness or heart. He used to love to go out and water our front lawn with the water hose in Temple City in the evening and have a beer. One time, my brother Bob and I were in the house watching TV on an early Saturday night, while my dad was outside watering. Bob and I were both good athletes who liked to work out with weights. We heard our dad yell at a car of teenagers to "slow down" as they raced down our quiet residential street. The next thing we heard was the brakes screeching, and this car was backing up in front of our house. These two young guys got out and started menacingly walking toward our dad. We were watching from inside the house. They were threatening him, but, to his credit, he was standing his ground. We decided to grab the two baseball bats and go out on the porch where our dad couldn't see us. We were hitting the bats into our palms as we stared down at the two skinny punks. They saw us and said something else to our dad, then wisely got in their car and took off. We went quickly back into the house and sat down, like nothing had happened. Our dad came walking in with a very pleased and confident look on his face and said, "That's right, those punks didn't want any of me." We never told him the truth, so please don't tell him.

I have contemplated writing a book about some of the experiences that have occurred in my life for many years. I think it took this long to finally fully appreciate the magnitude and widespread importance that these events have meant to my life. Everything I have experienced has shaped my existence and made me the person I am today. I am amazed at the range of experiences I have had and that this book has only minimally touched on over thirty-five years of teaching and forty years of coaching.

I lived through a tragic airplane crash for a reason. I truly believe it was to marry my wife, Laura; start a family; and have three wonderful children: Jonathan, Brian, and Kristina; become a teacher and have some kind of positive influence on my students (especially because I have mainly taught sophomores in high school, considering I was a sophomore when my plane crash occurred); and to be a coach for numerous sports (mainly high school girls and boys basketball, baseball, and softball). And maybe, to be an author…

About the Author

The author has been a public high school teacher and coach for the last thirty-five years across Southern California (including Los Angeles County, Orange County, and Riverside County). He has spent the majority of his career in the Desert Sands Unified School District in the Coachella Valley. He and his wife, Laura, have three children and have been married for over thirty years.